FaithWords

LARGE
PRINT

Worry-Free
LIVING

Trading Anxiety for Peace

——

JOYCE MEYER

LARGE PRINT

Unless otherwise indicated, all Scripture quotations are taken from the *Amplified Bible* (AMP). *The Amplified Bible*, Old Testament, copyright © 1965, 1987 by The Zondervan Corporation. *The Amplified New Testament*, copyright © 1954, 1958, 1987 by The Lockman Foundation. Used by permission.

Scripture quotations marked "NKJV" are taken from the New King James Version. Copyright © 1982 by Thomas Nelson, Inc. Used by permission. All rights reserved.

Scripture quotations marked "KJV" are taken from the King James Version of the Bible. The author has emphasized some words in Scripture quotations. These words are not emphasized in the original Bible versions.

Scripture quotations marked "NASB" are taken from the New American Standard Bible, copyright ©1960, 1962, 1963, 1968, 1971, 1972, 1973, 1975, 1977, 1995 by The Lockman Foundation.

Scripture passages or verses paraphrased by the author are based on the *Amplified Bible* or the King James Version of the Bible.

Derived from material previously published in *Be Anxious for Nothing*.

FaithWords

Hachette Book Group

1290 Avenue of the Americas

New York, NY 10104

www.faithwords.com

First Edition: June 2016
FaithWords is a division of Hachette Book Group, Inc.
The FaithWords name and logo are trademarks of Hachette Book Group, Inc.

The Hachette Speakers Bureau provides a wide range of authors for speaking events. To find out more, go to www.hachettespeakersbureau.com or call (866) 376-6591.

The publisher is not responsible for websites (or their content) that are not owned by the publisher.

Library of Congress Cataloging-in-Publication Data
Names: Meyer, Joyce, 1943- author. | Meyer, Joyce, 1943- Be anxious for
    nothing.
Title: Worry-free living : trading anxiety for peace / Joyce Meyer.
Description: first [edition]. | New York : Faith Words, 2016. | "Derived from
    material previously published in Be Anxious for Nothing."
Identifiers: LCCN 2016001567 | ISBN 9781455532483 (hardcover) | ISBN
    9781455566167 (large print) | ISBN 9781478909446 (audio download) | ISBN
    9781478909439 (audio cd) | ISBN 9781455532476 (ebook)
Subjects: LCSH: Anxiety—Religious aspects—Christianity. | Worry—Religious
    aspects—Christianity. | Peace—Religious aspects—Christianity.
Classification: LCC BV4908.5 .M495 2016 | DDC 248.8/6—dc23 LC record available at
    http://lccn.loc.gov/2016001567

Printed in the United States of America

RRD-C

10 9 8 7 6 5 4 3

CONTENTS

INTRODUCTION

———

Have you ever worried so much about things—or about one specific situation—that you lost your ability to enjoy your everyday life? Have you ever been so anxious or nervous that you completely forgot what it feels like to live in peace? If you answered yes to either of these questions, you are not alone. Many people struggle with worry and anxiety, but they do not have to! God wants us to enjoy our lives and to live in peace and rest, trusting Him with all our cares and concerns. I have written this book to help you do that and find your way to worry-free living.

As we begin, let's look at two key scriptures that are vital for us to understand and to live by if we want to live a calm, peaceful life:

Be anxious for nothing, but in everything by prayer and supplication with thanksgiving let your requests be made known to God. And the peace of God, which surpasses all comprehension, will guard your hearts and your minds in Christ Jesus.

Philippians 4:6–7 NASB

Therefore humble yourselves under the mighty hand of God, that He may exalt you at the proper time, casting all your anxiety on Him, because He cares for you.

1 Peter 5:6–7 NASB

These verses assure us that, for Christians, peace is possible and worry-free living is within reach. In fact, for believers in Jesus Christ, peace should be the normal condition in which we live our daily lives. But as I meet and talk with people, I realize this is not always the case, and I hope the following pages will help people understand and experience the peace God has provided for us, the peace in which He wants us to live each day.

We can see from Philippians 4:6–7 and from 1 Peter 5:6–7 that God tells us in His Word to "be anxious for nothing" and to cast all our care on Him. Although the words of these scriptures may be familiar to us, we do not always know how to apply them to our lives in practical ways. Sometimes, especially when a situation is very stressful, we are accustomed to responding to it as the world would respond, with anxiety or fear, instead of responding according to God's Word. When we do that, we end up muddling along in our circumstances, worried and nervous, when we could be enjoying the abundant life and peace God has for us.

I know firsthand what living in a state of anxiety and inner turmoil is like because I lived that way for many years. There were lots of days and weeks I had no peace at all! Only when I began to study the Word of God and apply it to my life did I begin to experience the peace, joy, and rest of God. I learned that God does not want His children to live in frustration, turmoil, worry, anxiety, fear, or confusion. When we allow ourselves to get caught up in these emotions, we are missing out on one of the greatest gifts God offers us, the gift of His peace.

Before we move forward, I want to share something with you about my journey from being anxious and upset to being peaceful and at rest because it may help you as you find your way to a new level of peace. When I first began living in the peace of God, as strange as this may seem, I was bored! I was so accustomed to being involved in some kind of internal uproar or mess all the time that I did not know what to do with the sense of calm that came to my life once I entered into God's peace. I can assure you, though, that boredom was temporary. It was simply an adjustment I went through as I left behind a life of strife, upset, and conflict and began to experience the peace God had for me. Now, I cannot stand to be upset or anxious about anything. I so love, enjoy, and appreciate the peace of God that has filled every area of my life. I work with the Holy Spirit daily to maintain peace in my mind, in my emotions, about my family, about my ministry—about everything.

I have challenging days just like everyone else does, but thankfully I no longer let them control me. The peace God has revealed to me is available to you, too. I pray that as you read and apply the words of this book, you will learn to cast all your cares on the Lord, because He cares for you, and to be anxious for nothing. A life without worry awaits you!

PART 1

YOU CAN CHOOSE PEACE

CHAPTER 1

Have a Glad Heart

All the days of the desponding and afflicted are made evil [by anxious thoughts and forebodings], *but he who has a glad heart has a continual feast [regardless of circumstances].*

Proverbs 15:15, emphasis mine

One definition the dictionary offers for *anxiety* is: "a state of uneasiness: worry…abnormal fear that lacks a specific cause" (*Webster's II New Riverside Desk Dictionary* [Boston: Houghton Mifflin Company, 1988], s.v. "anxiety"). This feeling of uneasiness, known as anxiety, is vague and its root cannot be easily identified. It is a general sense of fear or dread we feel without being able to specifically name its source. I used to feel this way often. I knew I had a problem, but did not know it had a name: anxiety.

I remember one particular season of my life when I seemed to be unusually plagued by anxiety. I was filled with dread over many things for no specific reason. I could not shake the fear that something bad was going to happen, but I did not know why. Finally I went to the Lord and asked Him what was troubling me. He brought to my mind the term "evil forebodings." At the time, I had no idea what those words meant or where they came from.

Sometime later, I ran across Proverbs 15:15, which says, "All the days of the desponding and afflicted are made evil [by anxious thoughts and forebodings], but he who has a glad heart has a continual feast [regardless of circumstances]." As I studied this scripture, I came to understand that I was like many other people. I was looking for some huge problem as the source of my anxiety, something big that was keeping me from enjoying my everyday life. In reality, I was just such an intense person that I created problems where no problems actually existed.

I had a bad habit of making a big deal out of nothing, getting anxious over things that were not worth being upset over, or as the old saying goes, "making mountains out of molehills." I finally reached the point where I realized I would stay anxious and upset all the time if I did not change. If I wanted peace in my life, I had to learn to just let some things go—forget them and move on.

The Bible teaches us that anxiety brings a sense of heaviness to a person's life. In fact, Proverbs 12:25 says, "Anxiety in a man's heart weighs it down, but an encouraging word makes it glad." I have certainly experienced the fact that anxiety weighs us down and keeps us from being lighthearted and free—and perhaps you have, too. Anxiety on a regular basis becomes a real burden and keeps us from enjoying life and moving forward in God's plans for us. People who allow their lives to consist of being anxious over one little thing after another do not experience much peace and joy. The good news is that we do have a choice. We can choose to be upset or we can choose to be at peace.

Thankfully, we don't have to live by our feelings, but we can learn to live beyond them or to manage them.

God's Word shows us there is a strong connection between Jesus and peace. When we choose Him, the Prince of Peace (see Isa. 9:6), we choose the way of peace. In John 14:1, Jesus said, "Do not let your hearts be troubled (distressed, agitated). You believe in and adhere to and trust in and rely on God; believe in and adhere to and trust in and rely also on Me."

Jesus also said in John 14:27:

Peace I leave with you; My [own] peace I now give and bequeath to you. Not as the world gives do I give to you. Do not let your hearts be troubled, neither let them be afraid. [Stop allowing yourselves to be agitated and disturbed; and do not permit yourselves to be fearful and intimidated and cowardly and unsettled.]

If we look at John 14:1 and 27 together, Jesus' message is clear. He made sure in these verses that we know we have a choice about whether to let ourselves get upset about things or not. We can control the way we respond to things that might trouble us. We can choose to be at peace or to live in turmoil. We can choose to stay calm when circumstances threaten our sense of well-being, or we can choose to calm down if we are getting agitated about something.

I want to be quick to say that although God's peace belongs to us as believers, our salvation does not guarantee a trouble-free life. We will still encounter problems and we will go through seasons in life when things do not work out the way we would like. Jesus warned us of this in John 16:33: "In the world you have tribulation and trials and distress and frustration; but be of good cheer... For I have overcome the world..."

Jesus knew that everything would not go exactly as we would like in our daily lives, which is why He told us we would experience tribulation. But Jesus also had an answer for it: "Be of good cheer," or in today's language, "Cheer up!"

Jesus, Who lives inside those who believe

in Him, has overcome the world and its troubles and tribulations. That gives us plenty of reason to calm down and cheer up!

Once I began to understand this principle, when I started to get upset about something that really did not matter, I felt the Lord reminding me, "Calm down and cheer up! Don't be so intense. Lighten up and enjoy your life!" Then I would think, *Oh, that's right, I am supposed to be enjoying my life. Joy is available to me through my salvation, and the Prince of Peace, Who has overcome the world, lives inside me!*

I encourage you to meditate on John 14:1 and 27. Begin to make the conscious decision to choose peace over anxiety. Remind yourself to calm down and cheer up! If you are like I was, the process of moving out of almost constant emotional upheaval and into a calm and restful place will take some time. But I can tell you from firsthand experience, it will happen if you stay committed to it. Living in peace is worth any amount of effort it takes.

CHAPTER 2

Rejoice in Today

This is the day the Lord has made; we will rejoice and be glad in it.

Psalm 118:24 NKJV

In Chapter 1, I mentioned one definition of anxiety and now I want to point out a second definition: *Anxiety* also means "to take thought" or to be "apprehensive, or worried about what may happen; concern about a possible future event" (*Webster's New World College Dictionary*, 3rd ed. [New York: Macmillan, 1996], s.v. "anxiety"). As I studied and prayed about the anxiety I struggled with for so long, I also began to think of anxiety in terms of my own personal definition: "Anxiety is caused by mentally and emotionally getting into things that are not here yet or things that have already been." This means we can become anxious anytime we leave the present moment and allow our thoughts to take us back to the past, which may cause feelings of anger, guilt, or regret, or allow them to take us forward to the future, which may result in the anxiety that comes from uncertainty.

When I first sensed the Lord helping me understand anxiety as I have just defined it, I began trying to be less intense and enjoy life. Like anyone, I still have problems, and although I may initially get upset or frustrated, I have learned not to stay upset about them. First Peter 5:8 states we are to be soberminded, vigilant, and cautious, constantly on guard against our enemy, who seeks to devour us. We can recognize and resist worry, anxiety, and being upset.

Many serious things are going on in the world, and we need to be aware of them and prepared for them. At the same time, we need to learn to relax and take things as they come without getting nervous or fearful. In spite of the troubling events taking place around us, we can learn to embrace each day, confessing and believing, "This is the day the Lord has made; we will rejoice and be glad in it" (Psalm 118:24 NKJV).

Many times, people miss the very first word of Psalm 118:24, which is *This*. When the psalmist writes *"This is the day* the Lord has made..." (italics mine), he is encouraging us to embrace and enjoy the present moment. Many times we postpone our rejoicing and being glad until we think certain circumstances are perfect. The fact is, perfection will never happen in this life; we will always be hoping for and praying about something.

If we wait until we think everything in our lives is just right before we rejoice, we will miss a lot of the joy and blessing God has for us. We need to learn to enjoy each day and every moment. Even when circumstances are difficult, if we can rejoice and be thankful in "this," whatever "this" situation may be, we will grow in spiritual maturity and we will be happier, more peaceful people.

One group of people who often say, "I

will be so happy when…" are young parents. I have heard this many times. Think, for example, about the hypothetical parents of a newborn son. They are overwhelmed by the needs of an infant, so they delay enjoying their child until he has reached a certain stage of growth. When he is an infant, they may say, "We will be so glad when he gets out of diapers!" "We will be glad when he can feed himself." Then, a few years later, they say, "We will be so glad when he goes to kindergarten." That soon becomes, "We will be so glad when he starts school." After several years pass, the parents say, "We'll be so happy when he can finally drive himself so we don't spend all of our time in the car taking him places." Then they say, "We will really be glad when he graduates." Then the child, who is now a young man, graduates and leaves home. The parents spent so many years waiting for certain milestones that they did not enjoy each unique stage of their son's life along the way. They were always waiting for *when*, and they missed so much of *this*.

I can certainly relate to this kind of thinking, *I will be happy when*... When I first started out in ministry, I had big dreams and small meetings. In those days, when only about fifty people attended our meetings, I often said, "I'll be so glad when I have hundreds of people at my meetings." Over time, I learned that nothing like that brings true happiness. I also discovered that each phase of development or growth comes with its own set of problems. I needed to learn to embrace each phase of my ministry, no matter how many people were in the audience.

Eventually, I did learn to be happy at each point and for every milestone along the way to the ministry I enjoy today. Years ago, I had a breakthrough when the Lord helped me really understand Psalm 16:11: "You will show me the path of life; in Your presence is fullness of joy, at Your right hand there are pleasures forevermore." True joy comes from seeking God's face (His presence). A familiar saying tells us to seek God's presence, not His presents (the things He can do for us). This is excellent advice.

To live in the fullness of the joy of the

Lord, we must find something besides our current circumstances on which to base our joy and gladness. The world is full of people and situations that will never please us. Even those people and things that do please us may do so only for a short time. Sooner or later people—even Christians—may disappoint or fail us, and circumstances will go against us. That's why we must learn to derive our happiness and joy not from what is going on around us, but from the Spirit of the Lord inside us. We need to learn not to fret or be anxious about anything but to give thanks and praise to God in all things (see 1 Thess. 5:18). This is a great way to stop worrying and start enjoying peace.

We will always have opportunities to be worried and fretful. The enemy will see to that because he knows anxiety weighs down our hearts (see Prov. 12:25), as I mentioned in Chapter 1. When he does try to make us anxious or upset, we can cast that burden of anxiety on the Lord with prayer and with thanksgiving, making our requests known to Him (see 1 Pet. 5:7; Phil. 4:6–7). Then the peace that passes all understanding will keep our hearts and minds in Christ Jesus (see Phil. 4:7).

People who think they will be glad when God does some particular thing for them may rejoice when they get what they wanted, but it is usually not long before once again they cannot be glad until He does something else for them. Then they become anxious about that next thing and they can spend their entire lives waiting for some other time to be glad, never experiencing the peace that is available each day. Psalm 118:24 teaches us that *today* is the day to rejoice and be glad, no matter what is going on or what we hope will happen tomorrow, next week, next month, or next year.

CHAPTER 3

Don't Worry, Seek God

Therefore I tell you, stop being perpetually uneasy (anxious and worried) about your life, what you shall eat or what you shall drink; or about your body, what you shall put on. Is not life greater [in quality] than food, and the body [far above and more excellent] than clothing?... But seek (aim at and strive after) first of all His kingdom and His righteousness (His way of doing and being right), and then all these things taken together will be given you besides.

Matthew 6:25, 33

Matthew 6:25–33 is a wonderful passage of Scripture in which Jesus talks to us about the

futility of worry and anxiety. Anytime we are
tempted to be worried or anxious, especially
concerning provision for our everyday needs,
we can find help and encouragement if we
will read and study these verses.

In verse 25, Jesus commands us specifically to "stop being perpetually uneasy (anxious and worried)." The fact that He gives us
such precise instruction is reason enough for
us to quit torturing ourselves with negative
thoughts and feelings. When we do that, we
are not only harming ourselves, we are also
overlooking one of the ways Jesus tells us to
live.

In Matthew 6:26–29, just after Jesus has
said to stop worrying all the time, He offers
a powerful example of what it's like to live
without anxiety about our daily needs:

*Look at the birds of the air; they nei-
ther sow nor reap nor gather into barns,
and yet your heavenly Father keeps feed-
ing them. Are you not worth much more
than they? And who of you by worrying
and being anxious can add one unit of*

measure (cubit) to his stature or to the span of his life? And why should you be anxious about clothes? Consider the lilies of the field and learn thoroughly how they grow; they neither toil nor spin. Yet I tell you, even Solomon in all his magnificence (excellence, dignity, and grace) was not arrayed like one of these.

Let me ask you: Have you ever seen a bird have a nervous breakdown or a flower droop its head with worry? Of course not! Birds and flowers do not worry about getting their needs met. Just as God feeds the birds and clothes the flowers of the field, so He will provide for those of us who put our faith in Him. We can trust Him for everything we need.

Jesus goes on in Matthew 6:30 to say, "But if God so clothes the grass of the field, which today is alive and green and tomorrow is tossed into the furnace, will He not much more surely clothe you, O you of little faith?" Think about this. You are of so much more value to God than a blade of grass, and yet

He takes care of it. How much more will He take care of you, His beloved son or daughter?

As Jesus continues His teaching, He says in Matthew 6:31–32:

> *Therefore do not worry and be anxious, saying, What are we going to have to eat? or, What are we going to have to drink? or, What are we going to have to wear? For the Gentiles (heathen) wish for and crave and diligently seek all these things, and your heavenly Father knows well that you need them all.*

We can find hope, peace, and confidence in the fact that God knows exactly what we need, and He promises to provide for us. If we take Matthew 6:25–32 seriously and believe the truth of this passage, we will realize we truly have no reason to worry about anything.

But Jesus does not stop with simply saying not to worry and making sure we know God will provide for us. He goes on to tell us how to use the energy we might have invested in being anxious. Instead of worrying, He says, "But seek (aim at and strive after) first of all His kingdom and His righteousness (His way of doing and being right), and then all these things taken together will be given you besides" (Matt. 6:33).

Seeking God's kingdom first is the key to living in the peace of the Lord. To seek God's kingdom simply means to seek to know God and His ways. We are to seek God's kingdom and His righteousness over all other things, and then everything else we need will be given to us as well. In other words, one reason we worry and fret and live in fear and anxiety is that we simply have our priorities mixed up. We are seeking our security in the things of this world rather than in the God Who created this world. God meets the needs of every created thing, including you and me! As believers, we are supposed to seek Him, not to seek the fulfillment of our needs. If we will seek Him first, He has promised to provide for us in every way, to open the doors of opportunity He has for us, and to give us the security we need.

For years, Dave and I lived on an extremely tight budget and I spent a lot of prayer time seeking God for financial blessings. At the time, even though we could have used extra money, I did not realize that I had needs that were even greater than my need for more provision. I needed to walk in love and display the fruit of the Spirit. I needed to be freed from selfishness, stubbornness, independence, and many other things. These are the things I should have been seeking, while trusting God to provide all the other things.

Through that situation I learned that God wanted me to believe He would bless us, but He did not want me to spend more time seeking financial provision than I spent seeking Him. By continuing to pray for and seek something that was not right for me at the time, all I was doing was slowing my own spiritual growth. Once I started seeking God above everything else and trusting Him to meet my needs, I realized that He always provided exactly what we needed when we needed it. He did not always give me what I *wanted*, but He did always meet my needs.

As I grew spiritually and began to value seeking Him more than I value anything else, all kinds of other blessings began to come my way.

Often, we spend more time seeking provision or other material things than we spend seeking God. Nowhere in God's Word are we told to spend our time and energy looking for the perfect mate, an ideal home, possessions, or a successful career or ministry. Instead, throughout the Bible, in both the Old and the New Testaments, we see the simple instruction to seek the Lord, trusting Him to provide for our basic, everyday needs and for all the other things He knows we need in accordance with His divine plan and timing for our lives. "Delight yourself in the Lord; and He will give you the desires of your heart" (Ps. 37:4 NASB).

CHAPTER 4

Enjoy Your Everyday Life

Peace I leave with you, My peace I give to you; not as the world gives...

John 14:27 NKJV

When Jesus said in John 14:27 that He gives us peace, He also said that His peace is "not as the world gives." As believers, we no longer have to live according to the standards and values of the world; we can live according to the priorities of God's kingdom. Jesus said in Luke 17:21, "The kingdom of God is within you [in your hearts]." This is true for all believers.

In Romans 14:17, the apostle Paul explains what the kingdom of God is: "[After all] the kingdom of God is not a matter of [getting the] food and drink [one likes], but instead it is righteousness (that state which makes a person acceptable to God) and [heart] peace and joy in the Holy Spirit." These qualities— righteousness, and peace and joy in our hearts—are characteristics of life in the kingdom, a life that is available to all believers. I can't think of any better way to enjoy our everyday lives than to live the lifestyle of God's kingdom by focusing on righteousness, peace, and joy.

When we think of the word *righteousness*, it may sound like something we could never achieve. Thankfully, it's not something we have to work for or something we can earn. It's a gift from God. Second Corinthians 5:21 says:

For our sake He made Christ [virtually] to be sin Who knew no sin, so that in and through Him we might become [endued with, viewed as being in, and examples of] the righteousness of God [what we ought to be, approved and acceptable and in right relationship with Him, by His goodness].

If we know Jesus as our Lord and Savior, we can be confident that He has made us righteous before God. To live in the kingdom of God means to be aware of the righteousness Christ has imputed to us. Another way to say this is that Jesus has made us acceptable to God.

Because of our personal relationship with God through Jesus Christ, we not only are made righteous, but also have access to peace and joy, which are listed in Galatians 5:22–23 as two of the fruits of the Holy Spirit. Though we always have access to joy and peace through the Holy Spirit, these qualities grow in us as we continue building and growing in our personal relationship with the Lord. Psalm 16:11 teaches us that in the presence of God is the "fullness of joy." The Bible also teaches us, in Ephesians 2:14 and John 14:23, that Jesus is our peace and He lives in our hearts. As we go through each day conscious of the righteousness, peace, and joy we have in Christ, we find ourselves more and more able to relax and enjoy our everyday lives.

The fact is, even though we are in Christ, we also live in a fallen world. We deal with all kinds of situations that try to steal our peace and joy—difficult relationships, challenging circumstances, and the enemy of our souls, who constantly seeks to destroy and devour us (see 1 Peter 5:8). The enemy does not always come against us in big, dramatic ways. He often opposes us by making us tense, getting our emotions tied up in knots, and causing us to worry, be upset, or feel disturbed and disquieted. He knows these negative thoughts and feelings will distract us from all the good things God has given us and is doing in our lives. The enemy knows that as long as we are not paying attention to God's goodness in our lives, we will not fully enjoy our relationship with the Lord and the abundant life Jesus died to give us (see John 10:10). We should always magnify the goodness of God in our lives above any difficulties that we experience.

Years ago, I wanted desperately to live in peace and enjoy my everyday life, but I could not seem to do it. In my case, I had many things from my past that still needed to be dealt with, and I had not yet learned how to truly trust God. I had many responsibilities and found myself unable to relax and enjoy life. Other people fail to enjoy their every-day lives for other reasons. Some are too anx-ious about little things or too fearful of big things; others are too busy and stressed; still others are trapped in the guilt and regrets of their pasts or in negative mind-sets that keep them from being happy even when happiness is available to them.

During my days of struggle, I could have enjoyed my life. I had a nice family, but I did not enjoy them because I wanted them to behave in certain ways. I was so busy try-ing to change them and make them who I wanted them to be that I often also kept them from enjoying their lives while I was not enjoying mine! I have learned through the years that other people are also blessed with great families, but do not enjoy them because they keep trying to change them instead of enjoying them while trusting God to make any changes that are truly needed. Think it over. Is there anyone in your life that you are trying to change? I can tell you from experience that it won't work. Only God is able to convict people of wrongdoing and convince them of right behavior. Pray and then wait for God to do what only He can do.

I also had a nice home, but I didn't enjoy it. I kept it spotlessly clean with everything in its place. But I was so determined to keep it neat and in order that I did not enjoy really living in it and I did not let others relax and enjoy it either. My children were young at that time, and they had some nice toys, but they were not able to enjoy playing with them because I did not want the toys strewn all over the house. I never wanted to get out the toys, get down on the floor, and play with the children. Part of that stemmed from the fact that I was abused during my childhood and I never got to really be a child. While much of my desire to control my surroundings came from my past, I realize that other people miss out on the enjoyment of their homes for other reasons. I have discovered that if people are unhappy with themselves, they usually blame it on their circumstances and the people around them. Freedom requires that we face the truth (see John 8:32).

Before I was able to enjoy my home, and all the other blessings God has provided for me, I had to learn how to enjoy myself, and I recommend the same thing to anyone who struggles with an inability to relax and enjoy their life.

I no longer dwell on the past or allow it to affect my happiness in the present, but I know that there was a time when I missed many opportunities to enjoy my everyday life. If you can relate to that, let me offer you hope by saying that if I could learn to relax and enjoy my everyday life, anyone can!

Whether you can relate to the intensity that kept me from enjoying my life on many levels or whether you are not enjoying your life for some other reason, I encourage you to remember that the kingdom of God is not having all the possessions we want, or perfect children or an immaculate home. The kingdom of God is righteousness, peace, and joy in the Holy Spirit. When the right things become priorities for you, you'll find yourself much less worried about the little things that can upset you each day and you'll be much better able to enjoy your everyday life and its everyday blessings.

CHAPTER 5

Overcoming Three Sources of Anxiety

Many evils confront the [consistently] righteous, but the Lord delivers him out of them all.

Psalm 34:19

Psalm 34:19 makes it clear that "many evils" will confront people who are consistently righteous. When we are in Christ, we are righteous (see 2 Cor. 5:21), so we know we will face challenges and difficulties. We may have lots of specific reasons to become anxious, but I think most anxiety comes from one of three general categories: the past and the future, conversations that haven't gone

well with others and confrontations, and the
duties and obligations of everyday life.

The Past and the Future

As I mentioned in Chapter 2, my personal
definition of *anxiety* is the way we feel when
we mentally leave where we are and start
thinking about an aspect of the past or the
future.

To be mature believers, we need to
understand that God wants us to be "now"
people—people who focus on and live in the
present moment. All of us live in the "now"
physically, but we often let our minds take us
back to the regrets of the past or move us forward to all the things we could worry about
in the future. We need to learn to live in the
present not only physically, but mentally and
spiritually, too.

As a simple example, I remember a time
when I was brushing my teeth. I suddenly
realized I was in a big hurry and feeling
tense. Although I was physically doing one
thing, mentally I had already moved on to

the next thing I planned to do. I was trying to rush through what I needed to do in the present so I could get to the future. No wonder I struggled with anxiety! I think I mentally lived one step ahead of where I was most of the time.

I also remember many days when I was a young housewife and I ended up frustrated every day trying to get my husband out the door to work and to get our children out of bed and off to school. Back then I spent a great deal of time frustrated because of all the things I wanted to accomplish each day. As a result, I was never able to concentrate on any one task for very long because I kept moving on to other things in my mind.

In the middle of doing one thing, I would realize I had not done something else. So I would stop to tend to whatever had come to mind and did not finish the first thing I had been doing. At the end of the day, I would be in worse shape mentally, emotionally, and physically than I had been when I started out that morning. All sorts of chores would be only halfway finished, and I felt totally frustrated, stressed out, and worn to a frazzle. On top of those negative feelings, I was also worried that the same process would repeat itself the next day—and it usually did.

I struggled as a young wife and mother because I neglected to give my attention and energy to one thing at a time. I finally concluded that one of the main reasons we find it so hard to focus on one thing at a time is that our thoughts tend to drift toward the past or the future rather than to remain in the present. Learning to live one day at a time relieves a lot of stress!

Ecclesiastes 5:1 says, "Keep your foot [give your mind to what you are doing] when you go . . ." In other words, we are to stay focused as we go about our lives. We need to learn to give our full attention to whatever we are doing. If we don't, we will end up anxious and worried because our minds will be constantly thinking about yesterday or tomorrow when we should be living today.

We don't need to be concerned about tomorrow because tomorrow will have problems of its own (see Matt. 6:34). We need to concentrate our full attention on today and learn to relax and enjoy the present. We can ruin today by worrying about the past or the future—neither of which we can do anything about. Let's refuse to waste our "now," because it will never come again.

The next time you are tempted to get anxious or upset about something, especially something in the past or the future, think about what you are doing right at that moment. Turn your thoughts toward what is going on today. We can learn from the past and we are wise to prepare for the future, but we need to *live* in the present.

Conversations and Confrontations

I spent many years of my life mentally rehearsing what I would say to people in certain situations. I imagined what they would say to me, and then I tried to figure out what I would say back to them. In my head, I practiced those imaginary conversations over and over. All of that going back and forth in my head caused a lot of anxiety.

Perhaps you have also carried on conversations in your head. For example, maybe you have imagined how your interaction with a boss would go if you asked for a raise or requested some time off to tend to a special need. People imagine all sorts of conversations with others, and if they are negative ones, they create a lot of stress.

When people are filled with anxiety about dealing with others, it may be a sign that they think the outcome of the conversation depends on them and their abilities rather than on the Holy Spirit and His abilities. Jesus told His disciples that they will face opposition for preaching the Gospel, but when that happens, the Holy Spirit will speak through them (see Mark 13:9–11). The same is true for us today. We do need to be prepared for certain conversations, but if we rehearse them excessively, we can fall into trusting ourselves and forget to trust the Holy Spirit. When we depend completely on God, He will work things out. As we trust Him to do so, we can stay at peace.

The Duties and Obligations of Everyday Life

You may remember the New Testament story of two sisters, Mary and Martha (see Luke 10:38–42). When Jesus went to their house, Martha was upset and distracted because she was overly occupied and too busy, while Mary sat happily at Jesus' feet, enjoying His presence and fellowship.

I can imagine Martha in this scene. I am sure that as soon as she heard Jesus was coming to her house, she started running around cooking, cleaning, and polishing, trying to get the house and a meal ready for His visit. The reason I find picturing Martha in these circumstances so easy is that I used to be just like she was.

One time my husband, Dave, and I invited some friends to our home for a simple barbecue. Instead of enjoying the process of getting ready and looking forward to spending time with friends over a good meal, I turned what should have been an easy backyard event into a major production. About that time, the Lord showed me something about myself—that I could not really enjoy my life because I made things so complicated.

A simple barbecue with friends became a stressful ordeal, all because I had the "Martha syndrome." I had "Martha" written all over me. I needed to learn to be more like Mary. Instead of worrying and fretting, I needed to learn to simplify my plans, lighten up, relax, and enjoy life.

All of us have tasks and responsibilities to fulfill every day. We can choose to be like Martha, flustered and upset, or we can choose to be like Mary, at peace and enjoying the presence of the Lord.

Whenever we start to feel anxious—whether it is because of something in the past or in the future, an upcoming conversation, or some type of obligation or responsibility—we need to remember that God is always with us. We can trust the Holy Spirit to help us in every situation, and we can relax and enjoy God's presence, His peace, and His joy in our everyday lives.

PART 2

YOU CAN LEAN ON THE LORD

CHAPTER 6

Two Sources of Strength

Thus says the Lord: Cursed [with great evil] is the strong man who trusts in and relies on frail man, making weak [human] flesh his arm, and whose mind and heart turn aside from the Lord.... [Most] blessed is the man who believes in, trusts in, and relies on the Lord, and whose hope and confidence the Lord is.

Jeremiah 17:5, 7

Anytime we face difficulties or obstacles in our lives, we have a choice. We can decide whether we want to draw our strength from ourselves or from the Lord. The Bible refers to two "arms," meaning sources of strength—the arm of flesh, which represents human effort and strength, and the arm of the Lord, which represents God's strength and power (see Ps. 89:13, 21). The arm of the flesh is rooted in our earthly nature and is based on human ideas and efforts; the arm of the Lord is rooted in the Spirit of the Lord and is based on God's plan and power. These two sources of strength are in direct contrast to each other, and will lead to vastly different results in our lives.

The prophet Jeremiah describes a person who leans on the arm of the flesh:

> *For he shall be like a shrub or a person naked and destitute in the desert; and he shall not see any good come, but shall dwell in the parched places in the wilderness, in an uninhabited salt land.*
>
> Jeremiah 17:6

Compare the description of that person to what the Bible says about someone who leans on the Lord:

For he shall be like a tree planted by the waters that spreads out its roots by the river; and it shall not see and fear when heat comes; but its leaf shall be green. It shall not be anxious and full of care in the year of drought, nor shall it cease yielding fruit.

Jeremiah 17:8

Many people strain and strive to get through every day, unhappy for reasons they cannot seem to understand or identify. Often, the cause is simply that they are trying to operate according to the frail arm of the flesh instead of trusting in the strong arm of the Lord. When we depend on the flesh and try to accomplish things in our own strength—coming up with our own ideas and using our natural energy to try to make them work—we end up frustrated and confused. But when we lean on the arm of the Lord—seeking what He would have us do and depending on His grace to help us see it all the way through—we end up satisfied and filled with joy over what He has done for us.

In Philippians 3:3, Paul writes strong words about not putting our confidence in the flesh: "For we [Christians]...worship God in spirit and by the Spirit of God and exult and glory and pride ourselves in Jesus Christ, and put no confidence or dependence [on what we are] in the flesh..." The flesh will always fail us, but the Lord will always be with us and see us through any situation to victory. Apart from Him we can do nothing (see John 15:5), but in Him we can do all things (see Phil. 4:13).

The Bible teaches us about two covenants—the old covenant, or the covenant of works, and the new covenant, or the covenant of grace. The covenant of works represents the arm of the flesh, while the covenant of grace represents the arm of the Lord.

The old covenant of works is based on human effort, while the new covenant of grace is rooted in God's divine enablement. One covenant brings bondage; the other brings freedom. Under one we bring forth the things of the flesh; under the other we give birth to the things of the Spirit. The covenant of works depends on the Law; the covenant of grace depends on faith.

The covenant of works depends on human strength, when people try to do everything on their own, struggling, striving, and laboring to be acceptable to God. Living under that covenant steals joy and peace. It's nothing but work, work, work!

The covenant of grace relies not on what people can do, but on what Christ has already done. Under this covenant, we are not justified by our works or attempts to be righteous, but by our faith and confidence in Christ. This relieves us of pressure to perform. Under the covenant of grace, we can give up our human efforts and rest in God's ability to work through us by the power of His Holy Spirit within us.

Under the first covenant, we wear ourselves out trying to make things happen on our own. Under the second covenant we enter into the rest of God and depend on Him to do for us what we cannot do for ourselves.

To fulfill the old covenant, we must be full of fleshy zeal. To fulfill the new, we must be full of God.

Everyone looks for a source of strength in something. You and I are either going to lean on the arm of the flesh, living under the covenant of works, or we will lean on the arm of the Lord, trusting in the covenant of grace. We will spend our lives trying to take care of ourselves or we will let God take care of us as we put our faith and trust in Him.

Colossians 1:4 offers great insight into what faith is: "For we have heard of your faith in Christ Jesus [the leaning of your entire human personality on Him in absolute trust and confidence in His power, wisdom, and goodness] and of the love which you [have and show] for all the saints (God's consecrated ones)." As part of our believing lifestyle under the new covenant, we act on what God tells us to do in faith instead of trying to figure out on our own how to solve our problems or how to reach our goals.

As believers, we need to rely completely on the arm of the Lord instead of on the arm of the flesh. To trust in the arm of the Lord means we lean all of ourselves on God, believing only He has the ability to do for us what needs to be done in us. Our only job is to abide in Him, to depend on Him totally and completely, to place our faith and confidence in Him. The arm of the Lord is the only source of strength that leads us to peace and blessings.

CHAPTER 7

God's Grace Relieves Frustration

[You should] be exceedingly glad on this account, though now for a little while you may be distressed by trials and suffer temptations, so that [the genuineness] of your faith may be tested, [your faith] which is infinitely more precious than the perishable gold which is tested and purified by fire. [This proving of your faith is intended] to redound to [your] praise and glory and honor when Jesus Christ (the Messiah, the Anointed One) is revealed. Without having seen Him, you love Him; though you do not [even] now see Him, you believe in Him and exult and thrill with inexpressible and glorious (triumphant, heavenly) joy.

1 Peter 1:6–8

Sometimes people say they lack joy in their lives because they have certain problems. I can understand why they feel that way, but I do not believe problems have to cause a lack of peace and joy because 1 Peter 1:6–8 says we can have inexpressible, glorious, triumphant, heavenly joy even *while* we suffer trials and temptations. If we can experience it when we struggle with trials and temptations, we can certainly experience these blessings in the ordinary circumstances of everyday life. No one enjoys having problems, but through Christ, we don't have to let them control our attitudes and actions.

If we are not enjoying the kind of joy described in 1 Peter 1:6–8, we need to ask ourselves why. Personally, I did not begin to experience joy despite my outward circumstances until I discovered the meaning of the covenant of grace, or leaning on the arm of the Lord, which I described in Chapter 6. The blessings of the covenant of grace were available to me, as they are to all believers, but I did not know how to live in them. As long as we live in ignorance or neglect the blessings that are ours under the covenant of grace, we will live in the frustration of works.

Even though grace is available to all believers, it will not benefit us if we never avail ourselves of it. Not only has God given us grace, He has also given us His Holy Spirit to be our Helper (see John 16:7) in any way we need His help and divine enablement. Unfortunately, not everyone is ready to receive help when they need it. Some people are stubborn and independent, preferring to do everything for themselves. At some point, though, these people realize they have exhausted every avenue of self-effort and come to the inevitable conclusion that whatever they are trying to do, they cannot do it alone. We have not because we ask not (see James 4:2), so ask the Holy Spirit to help you in all you do and you will experience less stress in your life.

I used to be like the people I have just described. I worried, fretted, and was anxious and frustrated over simple things. I recall once becoming frustrated because I could not get a jar of mayonnaise opened until I finally gave up and asked my husband, Dave, to open it for me. What made me act that way? Pure stubbornness! I wanted to prove I did not need anyone's help and that I could do things for myself. But I could not, and that frustrated me.

I believe works of the flesh always lead to frustration. As long as we live under the covenant of works, trying to do everything in our own strength, we will be frustrated and discouraged. Why? Because we are trying to do God's job. But if we live under the covenant of grace and trust the Lord to lead and empower us, we will live under the divine enablement God gives us. That does not mean we will never encounter trials intended to help us develop our character and test our faith; it simply means we will have the grace to go through any challenge and come out victoriously.

The way we receive God's help—and therefore avoid the frustration of works—is by simply asking for it. But people who are stuck in pride and stubbornness, as I once was, will not ask. Only the humble will ask for help because doing so acknowledges that we cannot do everything for ourselves.

Peter writes about the value of humility in receiving God's grace:

> *Clothe (apron) yourselves, all of you, with humility [as the garb of a servant, so that its covering cannot possibly be stripped from you, with freedom from pride and arrogance] toward one another. For God sets Himself against the proud... but gives grace (favor, blessing) to the humble. Therefore humble yourselves [demote, lower yourselves in your own estimation] under the mighty hand of God, that in due time He may exalt you, casting the whole of your care [all your anxieties, all your worries, all your concerns, once and for all] on Him, for He cares for you affectionately and cares about you watchfully.*
>
> 1 Peter 5:5–7

We can see from this passage that an attitude of humility is important to God. If we are full of pride and do things our own way without listening to Him, we will end up in situations that produce anxiety and stress.

God's reason for asking us to do things the way He asks us to do them is not that He wants to withhold anything from us or take anything away from us. Instead, He may be trying to set us up for a blessing. Or He may be trying to protect us from something we do not know about. We must always be on guard against pride because it will keep us from experiencing peace and joy in our lives.

I am reminded of a story about an encounter I had with a lady who attended one of our meetings many years ago, back in the days of cassette tapes. One afternoon after I had taught on the subject of pride and humility, she said to me, "I am looking for one of your teaching albums, but I don't see it on the resource table."

"Which one is it?" I asked.

"The one about exchanging pride for humility," she answered.

"We don't usually carry that one with us

at our conferences," I told her, "because there is not much demand for it. Those who are humble don't need it and those who do need it are too proud to pick it up!"

That story would be amusing if it were not true.

James 4:6 teaches us that God gives us more and more grace—power of the Holy Spirit—to overcome all of our negative tendencies. It says, "God sets Himself against the proud and haughty, but gives grace [continually] to the lowly (those who are humble enough to receive it)." Like Peter (see 1 Peter 5:6), James then urges us, "Humble yourselves [feeling very insignificant] in the presence of the Lord, and He will exalt you [He will lift you up and make your lives significant]" (James 4:10).

We receive God's grace by humbling ourselves before Him, casting all our cares upon Him, and trusting Him to take care of them as He promises in His Word. Those who humble themselves are the ones who get the help! A proud person will not humble himself or herself to receive God's grace. But those who walk in humility before God will receive the grace of God. That grace will enable them to avoid the frustration of works and live in peace and joy.

CHAPTER 8

Let God Build Your Life

Except the Lord builds the house, they labor in vain who build it; except the Lord keeps the city, the watchman wakes but in vain. It is vain for you to rise up early, to take rest late, to eat the bread of [anxious] toil—for He gives [blessings] to His beloved in sleep.

Psalm 127:1–2

Our society places a lot of emphasis and value on building a good life, including a career and a good reputation. When we try to build our lives and our reputations by ourselves, we are leaning on the arm of flesh. We work so hard to develop skills, find a career, earn money, build relationships, make a

good name for ourselves, and do everything
we think will cause us to be successful as the
world views success. But Psalm 127:1–2 indi-
cates that all this effort is in vain. The Lord
is the One who builds our lives and our reputations, according to the good plans He has
for us.

In Galatians 3:3–5, Paul reminds the
believers in Galatia of the difference between
trying to do everything themselves and allowing God to do what needs to be done; this is
the difference between faith and works.

*Are you so foolish and so senseless and so
silly? Having begun [your new life spiri-
tually] with the [Holy] Spirit, are you
now reaching perfection [by dependence]
on the flesh? Have you suffered so many
things and experienced so much all for
nothing (to no purpose)—if it really is
to no purpose and in vain? Then does He
Who supplies you with His marvelous
[Holy] Spirit and works powerfully and
miraculously among you do so on [the
grounds of your doing] what the Law*

demands, or because of your believing in
and adhering to and trusting in and rely-
ing on the message that you heard?

All of us would be wise to ask ourselves
the same question Paul asked the Galatians: Having begun our new lives in Christ
by dependence on the Spirit, are we now
trying to live them in the flesh? Just as we
were saved by grace (God's unmerited favor)
through faith, and not by works of the flesh
(see Eph. 2:8–9), we need to learn to live by
grace through faith and not by human effort
or works of the flesh.

When we were saved, we were in no condition to help ourselves. What kind of condition are we in now that we have been saved
by grace through faith in the finished work of
Jesus Christ? We are still in no condition to
help ourselves! Why then do we keep trying
to make things happen through the flesh?

The only way we will ever be "built [into]
a spiritual house, for a holy (dedicated, consecrated) priesthood, to offer up [those]
spiritual sacrifices [that are] acceptable and

pleasing to God through Jesus Christ" (1 Pet. 2:5) is by submitting ourselves to God and letting Him do in us the work that needs to be done. That is the only way we can become who and what God desires for us.

The flesh does us no good. We may realize that we need to grow and change in order to become everything God wants us to be and to experience all He wants us to enjoy. But we cannot change ourselves from who we are to who God wants us to be. All we can do is be willing to be changed and humbly submit ourselves to the Lord, allowing Him to build us into the people He wants us to be. The Holy Spirit works with us, helping us work out our salvation (see Phil. 2:12). We don't work for our salvation, but we do need to cooperate with the Holy Spirit in order to see it worked out in us.

We can be confident that God is working in us, changing us, and helping us grow through our faith in Him, so we can fulfill His good plans for our lives. In Philippians 1:6, Paul writes to assure us of this: "He Who began a good work in you will continue until the day of Jesus Christ [right up to the time of His return], developing [that good work] and perfecting and bringing it to full completion in you." You and I may have confidence that God will complete the good work He has begun in us!

What Paul is saying is simply this: God is the One Who started this good work in you and He is the One Who will finish it! This means we should allow God to do His work without trying to interfere. We need to be patient and rest in Him as He accomplishes what needs to be done instead of getting involved in things when they are not happening as quickly as we would like or in the way we would like. There are certain responsibilities we need to fulfill in our lives, but there are certain things only God can do. We are to do our part and let Him do His. That takes the pressure off of us, which relieves the worry and anxiety of trying to build our own lives.

Many times we let God work in certain areas of our lives, but we struggle to relinquish control of other parts. I believe this may be true when it comes to what other people think about us—in other words, our reputations. Paul writes in Galatians 1:10, "Now am I trying to win the favor of men, or of God? Do I seek to please men? If I were still seeking popularity with men, I should not be a bond servant of Christ (the Messiah)." In other words, Paul had to choose between pleasing God and pleasing people. That is a choice each of us must also make.

Philippians 2:7 says that Jesus "made Himself of no reputation" (NKJV). This tells us He was not at all concerned about making a name for Himself, and we need to follow His example. If we are faithful to God and humble before Him as we go about our lives, He will make sure the right people know who we are and He will open the doors that need to be opened for us. If our goal is to build a great reputation for ourselves, we will live as people pleasers who fear the opinions of others, rather than as people who fear the Lord.

For years I tried to build my own reputation among my fellow believers by trying to win their favor. At one point in my life, I manipulated situations and played all kinds of fleshly games to become popular and respected with a certain group of people in my church. Through a painful experience, I learned that if we are to be truly free in the Lord, we must do as Paul instructs in Galatians 5:1: "In [this] freedom Christ has made us free [and completely liberated us]; stand fast then, and do not be hampered and held ensnared and submit again to a yoke of slavery [which you have once put off]."

When it comes to letting God build our reputations for us, one thing we must be diligent to avoid is a feeling of rejection from other people. I do not think the enemy uses anything more than the threat of rejection when he wants to keep people from doing the will of God. When I committed to follow God's will for my life, many former friends abandoned me and some even turned against me. I soon learned I had to choose between pleasing people and pleasing God. Had I chosen to be popular with people, I would not enjoy the place of ministry I enjoy today. Are you letting the fear of man steal the destiny God has for you? If so, it is never too late to make a change and care more about pleasing God than about pleasing people.

Jesus' followers have faced this same choice for centuries. In John 12:42–43 we read:

> *And yet [in spite of all this] many even of the leading men (the authorities and the nobles) believed and trusted in Him. But because of the Pharisees they did not confess it, for fear that [if they should acknowledge Him] they would be expelled from the synagogue; for they loved the approval and the praise and the glory that come from men [instead of and] more than the glory that comes from God. [They valued their credit with men more than their credit with God.]*

Today you and I are faced with a decision. Are we going to keep trying to build our own lives and our reputations, or are we willing to give up all our human efforts and trust God with our lives? Are we ready to stop leaning on the arm of flesh and start leaning on the arm of the Lord? I tend to think this is accomplished according to the law of gradual growth. As we learn more about God and experience His goodness in our lives, we trust Him more and more. I trust God, but I hope to trust Him even more as time goes by.

CHAPTER 9

The Lord Brings Victory

You shall not need to fight in this battle; take your positions, stand still, and see the deliverance of the Lord [Who is] with you, O Judah and Jerusalem. Fear not nor be dismayed. Tomorrow go out against them, for the Lord is with you.

2 Chronicles 20:17

In 2 Chronicles 20, a large group of enemy armies came against the nation of Judah to drive them out of the land that God had promised them (see vv. 1–2, 7). Judah's King Jehoshaphat was a godly man and he led the people in seeking God for help and victory in a very difficult situation.

In 2 Chronicles 20:12, Jehoshaphat prays

to the Lord: "O our God, will You not exercise judgment upon them? For we have no might to stand against this great company that is coming against us. We do not know what to do, but our eyes are upon You." In this verse, Jehoshaphat makes three important statements that apply to us today as much as they did to the people of Old Testament times. First, he says, "We have no might to stand against this great company that is coming against us." In other words, he admitted that his army would be overwhelmed by their enemies if they relied on their own strength. Second, he confesses, "We do not know what to do." With these words, he acknowledged that the people were completely helpless, desperate for God's direction. And third, he declares, "But our eyes are upon You." He knew that God was his only source of hope and strength.

When we reach the point where we can say these same things to God in total honesty and complete dependence on Him, He can act on our behalf, as He did for the people in this story.

Sometimes we wonder why it seems God is not moving in our lives. The answer may be that we still have too much confidence in our own abilities and are still relying on the arm of the flesh in some way. The reason God may not be taking control of our situation is that we will not let go of it. This may be, in part, why 2 Chronicles 20:15 says the battle (representing the battles we face in life) is not ours, but belongs to the Lord.

If we look at this passage as a whole, we can see that before we get to the place where we can shout with confidence, "The battle belongs to the Lord," we have to do as Jehoshaphat did—recognize that we are powerless against our enemies and admit that we do not know what to do. Then we need to declare that our eyes are on God and that we trust Him to deliver us.

Once we stop looking to the arm of the flesh for help and for solutions to our problems, God will begin to give us instructions that will lead us to victory. Sometimes He will lead us to do specific things, but often He tells us to simply stand still. When He spoke to the people of Judah in the face of great opposition, He said, "Take your positions, *stand still,* and see the deliverance of the Lord" (2 Chron. 20:17, italics mine). In Psalm 46:10, God says, "Be still, and know (recognize and understand) that I am God." And in Isaiah 40:31 we read:

Those who wait for the Lord [who expect, look for, and hope in Him] shall change and renew their strength and power; they shall lift their wings and mount up [close to God] as eagles [mount up to the sun]; they shall run and not be weary, they shall walk and not faint or become tired.

During the battles we face in our lives, we would be wise to take some time and be still, waiting on the Lord to hear what He wants to say to us. In fact, we might even do absolutely nothing for a certain amount of time except fall to our knees and say, "Lord, I am waiting on You. I worship You and wait for You to move against my enemies and bring forth my deliverance." However, the type of waiting that God desires is not at all passive. It is spiritually active! We should be aggressively *expecting* God to move on our behalf at any moment.

During the Israelites' journey out of Egypt toward the Promised Land, the Spirit of God went before them in a cloud, leading them in the way they needed to go. Each time the Ark of the Covenant was lifted up, Moses cried out to God, "Rise up, Lord; let Your enemies be scattered; and let those who hate You flee before You" (Num. 10:35). I believe this should be our cry any time we face battles in our lives: "Let God arise and let His enemies be scattered!" When we understand that only God can solve our problems and we stop trying to do it in our own strength, we alleviate the pressure of worry and anxiety.

We must remember how great God is and never lose sight of His power. Sometimes we think of Him and His abilities from our limited human perspective and that causes us to lose sight of His greatness. We serve a mighty and all-powerful God. Every enemy will crumble before Him. He is infinitely stronger and more powerful than any enemy we could ever face, so we need to keep our eyes on Him instead of on ourselves. When we rely on our own strength, we lean on weakness and ultimately experience defeat. But when we depend completely on the arm of the Lord, He brings victory in every situation we face, just as He did for Jehoshaphat and the people of Judah.

CHAPTER 10

With Us Is the Lord Our God

Be strong and courageous. Be not afraid or dismayed before the king of Assyria and all the horde that is with him, for there is Another with us greater than [all those] with him. With him is an arm of flesh, but with us is the Lord our God to help us and to fight our battles.

2 Chronicles 32:7–8

Throughout the Old Testament, God's people faced opposition and fought many battles. In the previous chapter, I wrote about how King Jehoshaphat worshipped God and trusted Him for a seemingly impossible victory, and God gave it to him. Several chapters after King Jehoshaphat's account, we read that Jerusalem falls under siege again, this time at the hand of a different enemy. In this story, found in 2 Chronicles 32, the Assyrian king and his army came in great strength to invade Judah and lay siege to Jerusalem. By that time, King Jehoshaphat was dead and King Hezekiah ruled over Judah. He encouraged the people with this message, which I have paraphrased from 2 Chronicles 32:7–8:

> *Be strong and full of courage. Don't be fearful or discouraged because of our enemy, the king of Assyria, and the huge army with him. The One Who is with us is greater than all of them put together. The King of Assyria will fail, and we will be victorious, because he is depending on the arm of the flesh, but we are trusting in the arm of the Lord.*

We learn from this story that God wants us to know we cannot succeed in life by trusting in ourselves and our own human knowledge, wisdom, strength, and ability. We can succeed only as we trust in Him.

Many of us have heard the familiar saying: "God helps those who help themselves." Some people claim these words come from the Bible, but they do not. In fact, they are not scriptural. Of course, we must help ourselves in certain ways. For example, God does not send angels to clean our houses or our cars; we have to do those things ourselves. We also need to take responsibility for earning a living. God gives us wisdom and strength for these endeavors, but we have to apply our own strength in order to accomplish them.

The Bible teaches that God helps those who *cannot* help themselves and that we are not to depend on our own efforts, plans, and schemes to get us through this life and solve our own problems; instead we are to depend on Him. To say that God helps those who help themselves is not only not scriptural, but also misleading. The statement tends to make people feel as though they need to do all they possibly can for themselves before ever asking God to help them. This is simply not true, according to 1 Peter 5:5: "For God resists the proud, but gives grace to the humble" (NKJV).

Our enemy would like nothing more than for us to believe this worldly statement and spend our lives in frustration, trying to take care of ourselves instead of leaning on God. When we ask God to help us, He may work through another person to help us, or He may give us the ability to do what we could not have done without His help, or He may help supernaturally. But we often forfeit any help at all because we don't lean on Him.

King Jehoshaphat and King Hezekiah both realized they were totally dependent on God for their deliverance and victory over their enemies. You and I need to have the same attitude these Old Testament kings had. In the face of big problems, they looked to the Lord. Rather than looking at our past failures, our present frailties, or our future fears, we should be trusting in God's wisdom, strength, and power. We should be reminding ourselves that no matter how many problems we may face, the One Who is with us is greater than all those who oppose us. As King Hezekiah said, with them "is an arm of flesh, but with us is the Lord our God" (2 Chron. 32:8).

Let me remind you that Jeremiah 17:5–8 says those who put their trust in the arm of the flesh are cursed with great evil. They are like a plant in the desert—dry and destitute. They cannot expect good things in their lives. But those who put their trust in the unfailing arm of the Lord are blessed. They are like trees planted by rivers. They thrive and produce fruit, even during times of drought. No matter what happens, they will flourish and "shall not be anxious and full of care" (Jer. 17:8).

Deuteronomy 33:27 also speaks of those who trust in the Lord: "The eternal God is your refuge and dwelling place, and underneath are the everlasting arms; He drove the enemy before you and thrust them out, saying, Destroy!" This verse reminds us again that we can be confident the Lord will fight our battles and gain us victory.

As we seek the Lord and spend time in His presence, we are choosing to lean on His everlasting arms, rather than on the faulty arm of the flesh. This kind of life—the life of leaning on the Lord, knowing He is with us and goes before us to win our battles—is a vital key to finding peace and experiencing worry-free living.

We may often feel that we should only ask God for help with big things, but He cares about everything that concerns you and me. So whether you are in a major battle, or dealing with a minor irritation, put your trust in God and lean on Him.

PART 3

YOU CAN REST IN GOD

CHAPTER 11

Find Rest for Your Soul

Come to Me, all you who labor and are heavy-laden and overburdened, and I will cause you to rest. [I will ease and relieve and refresh your souls.] Take My yoke upon you and learn of Me, for I am gentle (meek) and humble (lowly) in heart, and you will find rest (relief and ease and refreshment and recreation and blessed quiet) for your souls.

Matthew 11:28–29

Just as we can be involved in all kinds of outward activities, we can also be involved in inward activities—feelings of joy, peace, strength, stress, anxiety, discouragement, or other emotions, positive or negative. These activities take place in our souls (our minds, our wills or desires, and our emotions). God wants us not only to enter into His rest in our bodies; He also wants our souls to enter into the rest and peace He makes possible for us.

To me, finding rest, relief, ease, refreshment, recreation, and blessed quiet for my soul means finding freedom from mental activity. It means not having to constantly try to figure out what I should do about the things that tempt me to worry or be upset. It means not having to live in the torment of reasoning, always trying to come up with answers I do not have. It means I resist the temptation to worry and instead choose to remain in a place of quiet peace and rest.

When something goes wrong in our life, rather than getting upset, we can speak to our soul and mind just as Jesus spoke to the wind and waves, by simply saying, "Peace, be still" (Mark 4:39 KJV). The Lord has taught me in trying times that I can "possess" my soul and rule over my emotions, rather than allowing my soul to rule over me. It is not always easy because I often want to merely do what I *feel* like doing, but I have learned that staying calm is actually easier than enduring what being upset does to me.

Jesus mentioned the idea of possessing our souls in Luke 21:19: "By your steadfastness and patient endurance you shall win the true life of your souls." In the King James Version, this verse says, "In your patience possess ye your souls." This is something we all need to learn to do.

I have always been the kind of person who likes to be in control, and I have never wanted things to get too out of hand. I like to plan my work and work my plan! Though I am much better now, I can remember many times in the past when I saw things begin to spin out of control in certain situations and I became upset. I had to learn not to let my mind and emotions get the best of me, especially concerning things I could not do anything about.

All of us have to learn to relax in situations we wish we could change, but have no control over. For example, suppose we are on our way to an important job interview and we get stuck in a traffic jam. How do we react? Is it worth getting all upset and unleashing our anger? Would it not be much better for us and for everyone else if we simply remained calm, cool, and steady, even if we were late for the appointment? I firmly believe, if we have done our best, God will do the rest.

Years ago, a lady came to one of our meetings in Louisiana. She told us she had just learned that her husband had been injured in an accident and was undergoing surgery in a hospital in Arkansas at that very moment. Yet there she was in the back of the church filled with the peace of the Lord. She couldn't get to him, so she chose to remain at peace instead of worrying, fretting, and being anxious. She could have been anxious and said, "Oh, why did this happen? Here I am trying to grow in my faith, and while I'm in church, a tree falls on my husband and causes a disaster in our lives. I just don't understand why such things happen to us believers!"

But the woman did not get angry or upset at all. She possessed her soul, and she stayed at peace. This lady set a great example for all of us. We need to possess our souls as well, refusing to allow our minds, our desires, and our emotions to rule our lives. If we don't, we will give in to anger or anxiety, giving the enemy a foothold to harass us.

Ephesians 4:26–27 says, "When angry, do not sin; do not ever let your wrath (your exasperation, your fury or indignation) last until the sun goes down. Leave no [such] room or foothold for the devil [give no opportunity to him]."

When we do not take authority over our own souls and we allow our emotions to run wild, we lose our peace very quickly. We certainly end up in inner turmoil and we often create strife in our relationships.

For example, Dave and I used to disagree about the silliest things. We often argued about what to watch on television after a long day at work. When we finally agreed on a movie we both liked, we argued about who the actors were.

Many times, we stayed up until midnight to watch the credits so I could prove to Dave that I was right.

As has happened many times, the Spirit of God eventually convicted me and showed me that in the big scheme of things, it really did not matter who was right or wrong because it was a trivial thing. God has more important things for us to spend our time on than arguing and losing our peace over something that unimportant. In order to keep peace while Dave and I watched movies together, I had to learn to bite my tongue and let Dave think he was right, even if I really believed he was wrong. The identity of a movie actor was not worth getting angry over and creating strife in my marriage. It certainly was not a good reason to give the enemy a foothold! Although this is a simple and possibly even a silly example, much of the peace forfeited in homes is over "silly" things that really don't make any difference when all is said and done.

So often, we allow our souls to get stirred up over situations that really do not matter. We blow things out of proportion and make major issues out of minor circumstances. If we want to live at peace, we need to learn to adapt and be flexible, to let things go, and to quit allowing our emotions to rule our lives.

When we become upset over insignificant matters, we throw open the doors of our lives to the enemy. We give him an opportunity to come in and wreak havoc. Often, the enemy does not have to do much at all to upset us, because we have developed a habit of responding to difficulty with some type of emotional outburst.

I believe we would be amazed if we truly realized all the Lord wants to deliver us from. As we choose to honor Him by possessing our souls and keeping ourselves at peace, Jesus promised that our souls would find rest in Him, and that rest is available to us every time we choose to live in it. Bad habits can always be broken by focusing on developing good habits, so I recommend that you start today to choose peace. Before long, your first response to turmoil will be to choose to hold your peace.

———

CHAPTER 12

A Place of Peace

Peace I leave with you; My [own] peace I now give and bequeath to you. Not as the world gives do I give to you. Do not let your hearts be troubled, neither let them be afraid. [Stop allowing yourselves to be agitated and disturbed; and do not permit yourselves to be fearful and intimidated and cowardly and unsettled.]

John 14:27

Just before Jesus went to the cross, He told His disciples He was leaving them a gift—His peace. After His resurrection, He appeared to them again, and the first words He spoke to them were "Peace to you!" (John 20:19). To prove to them Who He was, He showed them His hands and His side, and then said once more, "Peace to you!" (John 20:21). Eight days later, He again appeared to them, and once more His first words to them were, "Peace to you!" (John 20:26).

Jesus clearly intends for His followers to live in peace no matter what may be going on at the time. What He was saying to His disciples centuries ago—and is saying to us today—is simply, "Stop allowing yourselves to be anxious, worried, and upset."

Circumstances that can cause us to lose our peace have been around for generations. Anxiety is nothing new. Even the Old Testament psalmist wrote about it in Psalm 42:5: "Why are you cast down, O my inner self? And why should you moan over me and be disquieted within me? Hope in God and wait expectantly for Him, for I shall yet praise Him, my Help and my God."

When we begin to feel disquieted and downcast, we need to hope in God and wait in confident expectation that He will move on our behalf. He is our Help and our God, and His peace is ours if we will choose it.

I have said many times, "When we begin to lose our *peace*, we need to remember our *place*." What do I mean by that? I mean our place in God, the place we have with Him because of our relationship with Jesus Christ. Paul explains this in Ephesians 2:4–6:

> *But God—so rich is He in His mercy! Because of and in order to satisfy the great and wonderful and intense love with which He loved us, even when we were dead (slain) by [our own] short-comings and trespasses, He made us alive together in fellowship and in union with Christ; [He gave us the very life of Christ Himself, the same new life with which He quickened Him, for] it is by grace (His favor and mercy which you did not deserve) that you are saved (delivered from judgment and made partakers of Christ's salvation). And He raised us up together with Him and made us sit down together [giving us joint seating with Him] in the heavenly sphere [by virtue of*

our being] in Christ Jesus (the Messiah, the Anointed One).

According to Ephesians 2:4–6, we are *in* Christ and are seated together with Him. In Ephesians 1:20, several verses earlier, we see that Christ is seated at the right hand of God in heavenly places. The fact that Jesus is seated is a key point. If you and I are in Him, which we are, and He is seated, then we should be seated also.

Why is it so important that Christ is seated in heavenly places, waiting for the Father to place His enemies under His feet (see Heb. 10:13), and that we are seated there with Him? Ancient Jews would have understood this much better than we understand it today, so let me explain.

Under the old covenant, the Jewish high priest had to go into the earthly Holy of Holies once a year to make atonement for his own sins and for the sins of the people. He did this by sprinkling the blood of certain animals on the altar. In the earthly Holy of

Holies, there were no chairs because under the covenant of works, the people were not allowed to sit down and rest. The Sabbath rest would not be instituted until after Jesus had gone into the true Holy of Holies and sprinkled His own blood on the heavenly altar. We read about this in Hebrews 9:24: "For Christ (the Messiah) has not entered into a sanctuary made with [human] hands, only a copy and pattern and type of the true one, but [He has entered] into heaven itself, now to appear in the [very] presence of God on our behalf."

The entire time the Jewish high priest was in the earthly Holy of Holies, he had to be ministering to the Lord. God had even commanded that bells be attached to the skirts of his robe: "And its sound shall be heard when he goes [alone] into the Holy of Holies before the Lord and when he comes out, lest he die there" (Exod. 28:35). This is important because under the old covenant of works, the high priest had to keep moving while in the Holy of Holies (representing the covenant of works); he was not allowed to sit down and rest. The bells on his robe could be heard jin-gling as long as he was in motion; if the bells stopped ringing and the priest was still, the people would know he had made some kind of mistake and had died.

Once Jesus, the High Priest of the new covenant, finished the work of salvation through His shed blood, when He entered into heaven, His Father did not say to Him, "Stand up, Son, and keep moving." Instead, He allowed Him to sit down. Hebrews 10:-12–13 says, "Whereas this One [Christ], after He had offered a single sacrifice for our sins [that shall avail] for all time, sat down at the right hand of God, then to wait until His enemies should be made a stool beneath His feet."

That is the same message God has for you and me today. He wants us to know that in His Son, Jesus Christ, we are seated at His right hand. We have the privilege of enter-ing His rest. That is a part of our inheritance as children of God. Now instead of running around trying to please God and win His favor through works of the flesh, we take our place—seated in Christ—and find rest and peace in the midst of any circumstance through our faith in Him.

Sometimes when I feel myself getting upset and my peace draining away, I remind myself to "sit down." That is a creative way that all of us can remind ourselves to remain peaceful in the storm.

CHAPTER 13

Calm, Cool, and Steady

But understand this, that in the last days will come (set in) perilous times of great stress and trouble [hard to deal with and hard to bear].

2 Timothy 3:1

The world today fits the description Paul gives in 2 Timothy 3:1. In many ways, we are living in hard times: "hard to deal with and hard to bear." In verses 2 through 5 of this same chapter, Paul describes in detail some of the types of people who characterize the days in which we live—people who do not know the Lord. He says they will be "lovers of self and [utterly] self-centered, lovers of money...proud and arrogant and contemptuous boasters. They will be abusive (blasphemous, scoffing), disobedient to parents, ungrateful, unholy and profane" (2 Tim. 3:2). But this is not all; Paul's description continues all the way through verse 8.

People living in the environment Paul writes about in 2 Timothy 3 could easily lose their peace. But in 2 Timothy 4:5, Paul teaches us what our response should be to all the trouble in the world, all the trouble in our lives, and all the people who are hard to deal with or hard to bear: "As for you, be calm and cool and steady, accept and suffer unflinchingly every hardship, do the work of an evangelist, fully perform all the duties of your ministry."

This is a wonderful Scripture! It is exactly what we need to do if we want to live worry-free lives: "Be calm and cool and steady." To put this in terms of a familiar phrase, when we encounter the inevitable challenges or problems we all face in life, we are to remain calm, cool, and collected!

Sometimes, when trouble starts in people's lives, they panic and begin asking, "What do

I do? What do I do?" They are reacting to their problems emotionally instead of staying calm, cool, and steady, seeking the Lord for direction and following the leading of the Holy Spirit.

It is difficult to be led by the Holy Spirit when we are emotionally upset. He often speaks in a still small voice and it is much easier to hear if our souls are quiet. I often tell people that when they don't know what to do about their problem, they should keep doing the things they do know to do. When we are faced with challenges, there are certain things we know we can do—pray, study and apply God's Word, and stay in an attitude of worship. We should also trust God and continue being a blessing to others. Then, any specific instructions God desires to give us will come in due time.

Each time we need help from God, we must realize that the practical steps God leads us to take to handle one crisis may not be what we are to do to handle the next one. The reason something may not work more than once is that the solutions to our problems are not in the *procedure* we use; they are in the *power*—the power God gives us to accomplish what He directs us to do.

God uses different methods to bring breakthrough for different people and in different situations. One time Jesus healed a blind man by spitting on the man's eyes and then laying His hands on him twice (see Mark 8:22–25). Another time He healed a man blind from birth by spitting on the ground and making mud, which He rubbed on the man's eyes before sending him to wash in the Pool of Siloam (see John 9:1–7). On another occasion He healed a blind man by simply speaking a word (see Mark 10:46–52).

None of the *methods* Jesus used opened the eyes of the blind so they could see. What brought healing to them was the *power of God* flowing through Jesus. The different methods were simply different means Jesus used to release faith within each person to whom He ministered. The key to finding peace in any situation is finding the power of God, and the key to unleashing God's power is faith.

Hebrews 4:3 is a well-known verse that

talks about entering into God's rest, but the verse before that, Hebrews 4:2, shows us that faith is also necessary in order to enter that rest:

For indeed we have had the glad tidings [Gospel of God] proclaimed to us just as truly as they [the Israelites of old did when the good news of deliverance from bondage came to them]; but the message they heard did not benefit them, because it was not mixed with faith (with the leaning of the entire personality on God in absolute trust and confidence in His power, wisdom, and goodness) by those who heard it…

Sometimes the Holy Spirit may guide us to take specific action that will lead to the breakthroughs we need. I had experienced back and hip pain for more than twenty years. All that time I continued to go to the same chiropractor, who did help relieve my pain through adjustments, but eventually my situation got worse. I felt led to try a different doctor and he discovered my hip was not formed properly. After having a hip replacement, I am pain free and able to do things I could not do for many years. Whatever the Lord leads us to do, it will do us no good if we do not remain in the rest of God. This is because if we are not abiding in His rest, we are not operating in true faith.

There are times when people are led to pray with fasting for a period of time, or we might be led to ask a specific person for advice. But the main thing we should do is make sure that whatever action we take, it is Spirit-led, and that we are stepping out in faith.

Hebrews 11:6 tells us that without faith it is impossible to please God. None of the methods we use as we fight the warfare of rest will mean anything if they are not mixed with faith. If we do use our faith and act in obedience to the Holy Spirit's direction, God's power will be on whatever we do and He will lead us to victory.

CHAPTER 14

Peace and Rest in the Presence of the Lord

For we who have believed (adhered to and trusted in and relied on God) do enter that rest, in accordance with His declaration that those [who did not believe] should not enter when He said, As I swore in My wrath, They shall not enter My rest; and this He said although [His] works had been completed and prepared [and waiting for all who would believe] from the foundation of the world.

Hebrews 4:3

The importance of entering into God's rest through believing and trusting in Him, while refusing to become anxious and upset about things, cannot be overstated. I call it "the warfare of rest" because we can defeat what the enemy tries to do in our lives simply by staying at peace instead of getting agitated when circumstances frustrate or offend us.

According to Hebrews 4:3, rest is a place we can enter into. I believe it is the secret place the psalmist writes of in Psalm 91:1 when he says, "He who dwells in the secret place of the Most High shall remain stable and fixed under the shadow of the Almighty [Whose power no foe can withstand]." This secret place is the presence of the Lord.

When we are in the secret place of God's presence, we do not have to worry, fret, or feel anxious about anything. We may be in a troubling situation and our flesh may be screaming, "Do something!" But we can remain calm, cool, and steady (see 2 Tim. 4:5). We can relax and feel secure, knowing that in the presence of the Lord there is peace, joy, and rest.

Moses was a man who knew God's presence, but Exodus 33 tells us that Moses felt uncertain and hesitant at one point. God had given him the mission of leading His people out of bondage and toward the Promised Land, but God had not told Moses whom He would send with him to help him. In a state of uncertainty, Moses let God know that he wanted to experience more of His presence:

> *Now therefore, I pray You, if I have found favor in Your sight, show me now Your way, that I may know You [progressively become more deeply and intimately acquainted with You, perceiving and recognizing and understanding more strongly and clearly] and that I may find favor in Your sight.... And the Lord said, My Presence shall go with you, and I will give you rest.*
>
> Exodus 33:13–14

Once God assured Moses that His presence would go with him and give him rest, that was all Moses needed. He was then ready for his great challenge.

What was true for Moses is also true for you and me. As much as we would like to know God's plans and ways for us, all we really need to know is that His presence will be with us wherever He sends us and whatever He asks us to do.

Moses had a big job on his hands, so naturally he was concerned about it, just as you and I can be concerned about some of the things God has called us to do. But all Moses needed was the knowledge and assurance that God would go with him and help him. That knowledge should always be enough for us, too.

Over the years, Joyce Meyer Ministries has faced many challenges as we have tried to bring hope and healing to others. There have been plenty of times we were tempted to get upset, frantic, or anxious. But the Lord has taught us to do what Paul teaches in 2 Timothy 4:5, to be calm, cool, and steady. He has shown us that we must be adaptable and keep our eyes on Him, not on our plans. If things don't work out the way we would like them to, we have to stay relaxed and trust Him to show us how to move forward.

Too often when things don't work out as

people want them to, they get frustrated and make comments such as, "Well, that does it! Now my plan is ruined!" I understand this, because I made those same comments many times in the past. But I have learned that if God is the One who "ruined" our plans, we had the wrong plans to begin with. If the enemy ruined one plan, the Lord will give us another one, one that will be much better than the one that failed.

When we feel that something has gone wrong or gotten messed up in our lives, we need to resist the temptation to be anxious and upset, and run into God's presence. Every time we think something has gone wrong, we need to say from Psalm 91:2, "Father, You are my Refuge and my Fortress. You are my God. I lean on and rely on You, and in You I confidently trust."

Verses 1 and 2 of Psalm 91 describe a person who dwells in God's presence and trusts Him completely, and I will address these verses in greater detail in Chapter 15. Here, I want to focus on the remainder of the Psalm, which lists the many powerful promises of

God's protection and provision. I hope you
will read them and take them personally.

*For [then] He will deliver you from the
snare of the fowler and from the deadly
pestilence. [Then] He will cover you with
His pinions, and under His wings shall
you trust and find refuge; His truth and
His faithfulness are a shield and a buck-
ler. You shall not be afraid of the terror
of the night, nor of the arrow (the evil
plots and slanders of the wicked) that flies
by day, nor of the pestilence that stalks
in darkness, nor of the destruction and
sudden death that surprise and lay waste
at noonday....Because you have made
the Lord your refuge, and the Most High
your dwelling place, there shall no evil
befall you, nor any plague or calamity
come near your tent. For He will give His
angels [especial] charge over you to accompany and defend and preserve you in all
your ways [of obedience and service].*

*Because he has set his love upon
Me, therefore will I deliver him; I will*

set him on high, because he knows and understands My name [has a personal knowledge of My mercy, love, and kindness—trusts and relies on Me, knowing I will never forsake him, no, never].

Psalm 91:3–6, 9–11, 14

In the *Amplified Bible*, the footnote under Psalm 91 reads: "The rich promises of this whole chapter are dependent upon one's meeting exactly the conditions of these first two verses (see Exodus 15:26)." What are the "conditions of these first two verses" in Psalm 91? Basically, they are that we stay at rest.

As believers, all of God's promises belong to you and me. His promises depend on His presence, and in His presence, we find peace.

CHAPTER 15

Trust and Confidence in the Lord

He who dwells in the secret place of the Most High shall remain stable and fixed under the shadow of the Almighty [Whose power no foe can withstand]. I will say of the Lord, He is my Refuge and my Fortress, my God; on Him I lean and rely, and in Him I [confidently] trust!

Psalm 91:1–2

In Chapter 14, I made reference to several verses in Psalm 91. Now I want to look at that powerful Psalm in greater detail. As we saw earlier, verses 3–16 of Psalm 91 describe many of the blessings God has for us. In order to receive those blessings, we must meet the conditions of verses 1 and 2—dwell in the secret place of the Most High and "remain stable and fixed under the shadow of the Almighty."

Specifically, there are three aspects of Psalm 91:1–2 that determine our ability to receive God's richest blessings. First, we must *dwell*, which means "to remain...settle... continue...sit (down)" (James E. Strong, "Hebrew and Chaldee Dictionary," in *Strong's Exhaustive Concordance of the Bible* [Nashville: Abingdon, 1890], p. 52, entry 3427, s.v. "dwell," Psalm 91:1). Note that in the New Testament, Jesus tells His disciples, "Dwell in Me, and I will dwell in you. [Live in Me, and I will live in you.] Just as no branch can bear fruit of itself without abiding in (being vitally united to) the vine, neither can you bear fruit unless you abide in Me" (John 15:4).

Second, we should dwell in the secret *place* of the Most High, meaning a hiding place, a place of protection, a place with a covering over it so we will be kept safe from all our enemies.

Third, we should *remain* under the shadow

of the Almighty, meaning we must make the Lord our Refuge and our Fortress, our safe place. We do this by leaning on and relying on Him and confidently trusting in Him, and staying there. Sometimes, especially when we find ourselves needing to be patient and wait on God for something, we can be tempted to move out from under the shadow of the Almighty and look for refuge in other places. We need to resist this temptation and choose to remain in God's presence continually. It is helpful to me when I am going through something difficult if I verbalize my trust in God. I say often, "God, I put my trust in You."

I like the way my husband, Dave, describes what it means to dwell under the shadow of the Almighty. He notes that a shadow is a shade, a protection from the heat or the sun. It forms borders between the light and the darkness. In the same way, there are definite borders or limits within which we must stay if we are to remain under the shadow of the Almighty, under His protection against the world or the enemy.

When we are outdoors in the summertime, we can choose to stand in the shade or shadow of a tree, or we can choose to walk into full, direct sunlight. The shady place will usually be a lot cooler than the sunny area and will offer more protection against the damaging rays of the sun. Our lives with the Lord are similar. As long as we choose to stay under the shadow of His wings, we will be much more comfortable and much better protected against danger than when we choose to step out from underneath God's protection.

We can choose to live under one set of conditions or under another. The wise thing is not only to choose to remain under the shadow of the Almighty, but to take up residence there, not venturing out from under the protection God offers us.

When we drive down a highway, as long as we stay within the lines that divide the lanes and obey the signposts along the road, we are in much less danger of being involved in an accident than if we ignore those boundaries and instructions. Those lines and signs are put in place for our benefit and protection.

Spiritually speaking, the "lines and signs" that keep us in the way of the Lord and out of danger are trust and confidence. As long as we place our trust and confidence in Him, He will keep us in His shadow and protect us from any real danger and harm.

After we read Psalm 91:1–2, we see that verse 3 begins with a critical phrase: "For then." It says, "For [then] He will deliver you…" When we carry out the instructions of verses 1 and 2, then the Lord will fulfill the wonderful promises of protection set forth in the remaining verses of the Psalm. We read in verses 3 through 7 that the Lord will deliver us (v. 3), cover us (v. 4), keep us from fear and terror (v. 5), and protect us against evil plots and slander (v. 5). We will have no fear of pestilence, destruction, or sudden death (v. 6), even though others may be falling as a result of these things all around us (v. 7).

Psalm 91:9–13 shows us clearly that the Lord promises angelic protection and deliverance to those who serve Him and are walking in obedience to Him. Verse 13 says, "You shall tread upon the lion and adder; the young

lion and the serpent shall you trample under-
foot." Jesus makes a similar statement to
His disciples in Luke 10:19: "Behold! I have
given you authority and power to trample
upon serpents and scorpions, and [physical
and mental strength and ability] over all the
power that the enemy [possesses]; and nothing shall in any way harm you." These words
describe our place in God. As believers, we
are in a position of power and authority over
the enemy and his demons and devices. We
also are in a position of favor and influence
with God.

Saying we have angelic protection does
not mean we will never experience any trials
or afflictions. It means we are protected from
what the enemy ultimately has planned for
us as long as we keep our trust in God and
believe and speak of Him in accordance with
His Word.

One important thing we must learn about
this angelic protection and deliverance is
that it is a *process*. The Lord promises us in
Psalm 91:15 that when we call on Him, He
will answer us and be with us in our troubles;

He will strengthen us and accompany us through our difficulties to victory, deliverance, and honor. It took me many years to see the following pattern: God is with me in my trials and troubles, then He begins to deliver me out of them, and afterward He honors me. This is a progression, and we will find peace and joy in the Lord as we go through it.

Psalm 91:14–16 assures us that because of our personal knowledge of God and of His mercy, love, and kindness, and because we trust and rely on Him, knowing He will never leave us or forsake us, we have been given His precious promises. These promises include the fact that He will be with us, answer us, deliver us, and honor us with long and abundant life. These assurances give us great peace and enable us to live without worry.

PART 4

YOU CAN TRUST GOD'S PLAN

CHAPTER 16

God Knows Best

In all your ways know, recognize, and acknowledge Him, and He will direct and make straight and plain your paths.

Proverbs 3:6

Three words that should relieve us of the anxiety and care we often feel about situations in our everyday lives are these: *God knows best.* Only in God's presence can we find the peace and joy we long for (see Ps. 16:11; 27:4).

Proverbs 3:6 teaches us that if we acknowledge the Lord in all our ways, He will direct our paths. What does it mean to acknowledge Him in all our ways? It means seeking Him for His direction and submitting all our plans to Him to work them out according to His will and desire for us.

One sign of spiritual maturity is to seek God for Who He is, not just for what He can do for us. Let me explain this using an example from an earthly relationship. If my husband returned from a long trip away from home, I would meet him and be thrilled to see him. He would be glad to see me, too, and he might even bring me a gift. Because I care about him, he delights in giving me things to show me his love. But if I met him after a trip and was more excited about finding out what kind of gift he brought me than about being reunited with him, he might be hurt. In contrast, if he saw that I was genuinely happy to see him and wanted nothing more than to be with him and enjoy his company, he would be glad to give me a gift.

When we acknowledge God in all our ways and seek Him for Who He is, we begin to want what He wants for us more than the things we once wanted for ourselves. His will starts to become our will. I have learned this from personal experience. I used to want what I wanted more than anything else, but now I want God's will more than my own. I know if I want something and God says no, it may hurt my feelings and be hard for me to accept for a while, but it will be better for me in the long run.

One time Dave and I were on vacation, sitting in our golf cart making plans for our next vacation. We were having such a good time that I was already planning our return to the same place the next year. Suddenly, the Lord brought to mind the words of James 4:13–15.

Come now, you who say, Today or tomorrow we will go into such and such a city and spend a year there and carry on our business and make money. Yet you do not know [the least thing] about what may happen tomorrow. What is the nature of your life? You are [really] but a wisp of vapor (a puff of smoke, a mist) that is visible for a little while and then disappears [into thin air]. You ought instead to say, If the Lord is willing, we shall live and we shall do this or that [thing].

When the Lord impressed those verses on me, He was not trying to get me to stop planning for the future. He was simply teaching me not to get ahead of His timing or to make my own plans in pride without consulting Him. His will and His purposes are what really matter. I should have been focused on what He wanted for our next vacation, not what I wanted. In that situation, I learned again that the flesh profits nothing and realized I needed to respect and honor God by seeking Him for His plans, not coming up with my own idea and asking Him to bless it. God often lets us do what we desire to do, but He does want to be acknowledged in it!

An important key to the abundant, joyful, peaceful life Jesus died to give us is humility. I mentioned in an earlier chapter that we need to learn to humble ourselves under the "mighty hand of God" so He may exalt us in due time (1 Pet. 5:6). One way we humble ourselves is by acknowledging God and waiting on Him, refusing to move in the energy of the flesh. We need to learn to live one day at a time, being content where we are and with what we have until the Lord leads us to something better.

The real issue was not the vacation I wanted; it was my attitude. Had my attitude been right, I would have begun lifting my heart to the Lord, saying something like, "Lord, if it is all right with You, I would really like to come back to this same place next year. We are starting to make plans, but if You do not approve, we will be happy for You to interrupt our plans and change them. We want Your will, not ours!"

I would not say that planning a vacation—or moving to a new house, returning to college, starting a business, or preparing anything else that requires planning and forethought—is wrong. But planning those things on our own, in the flesh, can get very frustrating and is not the best way. The best way is to acknowledge and honor God, leaning on Him as our source of strength. We can eliminate a lot of worry in our lives if we really believe that God knows best and simply trust in Him. A minister that I know who has been in ministry for more than fifty years recently told me that three times a day he takes a few minutes and asks the Holy Spirit to guide him in all that he does, and to let him know if he is doing anything that is not God's will. This is the type of attitude that God wants us to live with!

CHAPTER 17

A Key to Being Used by God

We possess this precious treasure [the divine Light of the Gospel] in [frail, human] vessels of earth, that the grandeur and exceeding greatness of the power may be shown to be from God and not from ourselves.

2 Corinthians 4:7

If you have ever felt that you lack purpose and value in life, you know that feeling produces a lot of anxiety. You worry about whether you are missing God's plan for your life. You may even wonder if something is wrong with you—and you worry about that. You may feel anxious because you want a fulfilling life and you want to please God and do His will, but that feeling of worthlessness leaves you unsure of what to do.

You may remember the Old Testament story of a widow who was so much in debt that her creditors came to take her two sons into slavery (see 2 Kings 4:1–7). When Elisha the prophet asked her if she had anything of value in her house, she replied, "Your handmaid has nothing in the house except a jar of oil" (2 Kings 4:2). Elijah said, "Go around and borrow vessels from all your neighbors, empty vessels—and not a few. And when you come in, shut the door upon you and your sons. Then pour out [the oil you have] into all those vessels, setting aside each one when it is full" (2 Kings 4:3–4).

When the woman had collected as many empty vessels as she could find, she did exactly as Elisha had instructed. She and her sons went into their house and closed the door. Her sons took each vessel to her and she filled all of them with oil. God multiplied her small amount of oil, and the flow of oil did not stop until she ran out of vessels. When the woman told Elisha what had happened, he told her to sell the oil and pay her debt, and to use whatever money was left for living expenses for her and her sons.

I share this story to make the point that all of us are empty vessels. None of us has anything of any value within ourselves except the power of God that can flow out of us. The key to becoming full vessels that God can use is found in knowing who we are in Jesus; this is the secret of our value and worth. When we know this, there is nothing for us to do but stand in awe of the Lord and give Him thanks and praise for what He has done for us in Christ. The first step to fullness is recognizing that we are empty when we look at ourselves in human terms.

Our value comes from the Lord. He assigns tremendous worth to each one of us through the blood of His Son Jesus Christ. We have nothing, and we are nothing, in and of ourselves. But in Christ, we have everything and we are everything.

When I first started ministering, I wanted to help people. I still remember the words the Lord impressed on my heart in those early days: "When you are empty of yourself so that all you have left within you is the ability to depend on the Holy Spirit, when you have learned that everything you are and everything you have comes from Him, then I'll send you around to your neighbors to fill their empty vessels with the life I have poured into your empty vessel."

Arriving at the place of being empty of ourselves is not an easy task and is rarely a quick one. A deep work must be done in each of us before we can say what the apostle Paul says in Galatians 2:20:

> *I have been crucified with Christ [in Him I have shared His crucifixion]; it is no longer I who live, but Christ (the Messiah) lives in me; and the life I now live in the body I live by faith in (by adherence to and reliance on and complete trust in) the Son of God, Who loved me and gave Himself up for me.*

I spent many years wondering if I would ever reach the point of being totally dependent on God instead of being independent, of trusting the Lord instead of my flesh. If you have ever felt that way, let me encourage you that as long as you don't give up, you are making progress. If reaching that place of dependence and surrender seems to be taking a long time, remember that God Who began a good work in you will be faithful to complete it (see Phil. 1:6).

If we press on and are sincere about spiritual maturity, we will eventually be like the woman in 2 Kings 4—empty of ourselves and ready for God to use us to fill those around us and to fulfill His plans for our lives. Only when we realize it is the Lord working through us—not anything we can do in our own strength—can we begin to serve Him and help others as we should.

To know and experience what God can do, we must first realize what we cannot do and be at peace with that. If we will stop trying to win the battles we face in life with our own strength and stop trying to use human effort to accomplish what we think we need to do, we will find the arm of the Lord moving on our behalf and doing for us what we could never do on our own. When we empty ourselves and truly realize that we are utterly dependent on God, He will fill us and move through us in amazing ways.

CHAPTER 18

There's a Time for Everything

To everything there is a season, and a time for every matter or purpose under heaven.

Ecclesiastes 3:1

One reason many people worry and become upset is that they want certain developments to take place at a certain time. When those things do not happen, people get frustrated and anxious, asking, "Will it *ever* happen?"

I believe the enemy offers us two lies concerning issues of timing in our lives—the "forever" lie and the "never" lie. When we face negative circumstances, he makes us think they will go on *forever*, and that things will *never* change. Both of these lies create worry and fear in our hearts. And both are untrue because, sooner or later, everything in life changes.

The difficulties we encounter won't last forever, and even the good things we enjoy in our lives may not stay the same forever. It is important for us to learn to adapt ourselves to seasons of change because they are part of the process of spiritual maturity. Difficulties will eventually give way to victory, and good times will become better times. Only God never changes, but everything else does—and we don't have to be afraid of change!

During such times, we can remember Psalm 91:14–16, in which God gives us powerful promises for changing times. Talking about a person who trusts and believes in God, these verses say:

> *Because he has set his love upon Me, therefore will I deliver him; I will set him on high, because he knows and understands My name [has a personal knowledge of My mercy, love, and kindness—trusts and relies on Me, knowing I will never*

forsake him, no, never]. He shall call upon Me, and I will answer him; I will be with him in trouble, I will deliver him and honor him. With long life will I satisfy him and show him My salvation.

I believe the message God is giving us in these verses is simply this: No matter what we are going through at any given moment, sooner or later it will pass. In the meantime, we can count on Him to be with us, to deliver us and honor us, and to satisfy us with long life and show us His salvation. Everyone faces some trials and tribulations at some point in life, but as we continue to believe God and place our trust in Him, He will fulfill His promises to us and those troubled times will give way to better days.

As our lives go on, we may run into other hardships along the way, but eventually, through Christ, those challenges will work out for our good. Whatever exists in our lives now, or will exist in the future, will be temporary because life is a continual process in which nothing stays the same. If we can grasp this truth, it will help us make it through any problems we face and it will help us appreciate the good times and seasons of blessing without thinking, *I just won't be able to go on if this never changes.*

As a simple example, consider this: If you have never had a nice vacation, the enemy wants you to think you will never get to go on one. On the other hand, if you are on vacation and enjoying it, the enemy wants you to dread that it will come to an end and he will make you miserable with thoughts of going back to work. In some circumstances, he wants you to believe things will never change, while in other situations he wants you to believe they will change, but you will be unhappy when those changes come.

Yes, things are always changing. Sometimes changes are exciting and you are full of joy; sometimes they are difficult or painful. Either way, we can make it through the changes of life without worrying or becoming fearful or upset if we keep our eyes on Jesus. Hebrews 13:8 says, "Jesus Christ (the Messiah) is [always] the same, yesterday, today,

[yes] and forever (to the ages)." He never, ever changes! In a world filled with change, He is the one constant.

As believers, our attachment is to be to the Lord alone—not to the blessings He gives us. God certainly wants us to enjoy the things He provides for us while we have them, but He does not want us to reach the point where we think we could not be happy without them.

We are stewards, not owners, of everything God has given us. As a personal example, I recognize that the ministry I am involved in is not my ministry; it is God's. If He ever decides He is finished with it, it will be finished. I expect to be involved in this ministry as long as I possibly can, but if God should ever let me know that He wants to bring it to a conclusion, then that is what will happen and I am prepared for it.

The same is true for you. None of us should ever grow too attached to our jobs, sources of income, possessions, hobbies, or human relationships. We must always be free to follow God's direction and move as the Spirit leads us. According to Ecclesiastes 3:1, there is a time and a season for everything, and when each season is complete, we must let go of the things involved in it. Too often we hurt ourselves because we try to hang on to the past when God is saying, "It's time to move on to something new."

Many years ago, Dave and I felt God's will for our lives was for us to begin training for ministry. The season we had been in was over, and God was calling us into something new. The first step we took was to enroll in a nine-month-long Bible class at our church. The course met two or three nights a week, which was quite a commitment because our lives were very busy at the time.

The course seemed like a major undertaking until God helped me understand something about reaching goals in life. I realized that a goal is like a horizon. We know what it is and we move toward it, but as we get closer, it fades from sight and a new horizon comes into view.

What God was teaching me through the example of the horizon is that we will always be moving toward some type of goal or objective. As soon as we reach one, another one comes up. God continually gives us things for which we can trust Him and believe Him, keeping us on a journey of faith. What we are believing God for today may manifest a year from now and we will be trusting Him for something else. He takes us from one season to the next. When He brings one season to an end because it has accomplished its purpose, we would be wise to allow Him to bring closure to that situation so we can fully enter into the next new thing He has for us.

If a season in your life is changing, let me encourage you to be willing to let it go. Look for the new thing He has for you and allow it to come to pass. Don't live in the past when God has something fresh and new for you. Let go of what lies behind you and press on to what lies ahead (see Phil. 3:13–14). If God is no longer involved in something or giving you grace for it, you will no longer be happy or at peace with it. Reach out toward that new horizon, knowing that with God, there is a time and a season for every purpose He has for you. As you trust His timing and follow Him from one season to another, you can enjoy each phase of life without worrying about the next one.

CHAPTER 19

———

God Has a Plan

Believe in the Lord Jesus Christ [give yourself up to Him, take yourself out of your own keeping and entrust yourself into His keeping] and you will be saved.

Acts 16:31

When God set Paul free from prison in Philippi, his jailer asked him, "What must I do to be saved?" (Acts 16:30 NKJV). In the next verse, Paul answered, "Believe in the Lord Jesus Christ," and then he explained what salvation really means—giving ourselves up to God, taking ourselves out of our own keeping, and entrusting ourselves to His keeping and care.

God wants to take care of us. We can make that much easier if we avoid a problem called independence, or trying to handle everything on our own. Our feeling that we must take care of ourselves is rooted in fear. It stems from the idea that if we do it, we can be sure it will be done right, or at least done in a way that makes us happy. Often, whether we are willing to admit it or not, we are afraid of what might happen if we entrust ourselves totally to God and He does not come through for us as we think He should.

The root of the problem with independence is in trusting ourselves more than we trust God. If we choose to trust God, we also might have a tendency to want a backup plan. What we may fail to realize is that God has a plan, too, a plan that is much better than any we could come up with for ourselves.

Independence is a symptom of spiritual immaturity. Just as small children try to do everything for themselves—tie their own shoelaces, dress themselves, or reach the cookie jar—instead of asking for help when they need it, immature Christians will also try to do things on their own, resisting the help God so willingly offers.

Sometimes it seems that God absolutely will not allow us to help ourselves when we face problems and struggles. The reason this happens is that God wants to help us, but He wants to do it His way, not our way—because our way usually involves worry, anxiety, reasoning, and excessive plotting and planning. God says in Jeremiah 29:11, "For I know the thoughts and plans that I have for you, says the Lord, thoughts and plans for welfare and peace and not for evil, to give you hope in your final outcome." He knows what His plans are, and He knows that His way is the best way to bring them to pass in our lives.

I learned this truth in a powerful way years ago through a letter a woman sent to our ministry after one of our conferences. Her wonderful testimony of freedom from self-care and anxiety is amazing. I would like to share some of it with you because I think it speaks to all of us.

When I came to your conference, I was anxious because I felt my life was not going to amount to anything for God, and I was afraid that no matter what happened, I was never going to be happy. I had been frustrated and unhappy for about a year and I really needed a breakthrough.

During the conference I felt God lifting me from many of my worries and cares. I felt a little better after each session. But when I would return home between sessions, those same anxious thoughts would attack me all over again.

Finally, after your last session, I decided that I could not face another day feeling so anxious and fearful. I bought your teaching series, Facing Fear and Finding Freedom, Be Anxious for Nothing, *and* How to Be Content. *I did not have money set aside for those purposes, so then I got worried about how to pay for the other things I needed money for.*

After I left the conference, I put one of the teachings in my car cassette player in hopes that my fears would not attack me again before I got home.

I stopped at a gas station and realized I did not have any money left. So I decided to use my debit card, which accessed an account containing my rent money, and to transfer money to cover the gas purchase into that account later that day.

When I arrived at the gas station, I made sure they accepted the type of card I wanted to use. I filled my tank and gave the attendant my card. He ran the card three times, and each time, it was denied. I had no other way to pay for the gas. By then I was perspiring, hyperventilating, and envisioning myself working for the gas station to pay back the amount of fuel I put in my car. I thought my life was over!

But then four women in a van pulled into the station. One of them got out and asked me if anything was wrong. Of course, I told her I was fine and thanked her for asking. I guess the panicked look on my face gave me away, and she insisted on helping me. Finally, I told her I needed money to pay for my gas, and immediately she and the three other ladies handed me enough money to pay the bill, and they drove away.

After paying for the gas, I returned to my car, relieved. When I started the engine, I sensed the Holy Spirit teaching me a lesson. He showed me that I spent my entire life planning. It was true. I got up every morning and I planned my day. While I brushed my teeth, I planned what I would wear. During the day, I planned for the evening. I planned what I would eat, what I was going to watch on television, when I was going to exercise—plan, plan, plan! I felt as though the Lord spoke to me and said, "You even planned how you were going to pay for your gas, and look where that got you."

Then He paused and impressed these words strongly on my heart, "I have a plan."

Although making plans is not wrong, sometimes we have to lay down our plans in order to perceive God's plan. I believe it is wise to plan our work and work our plan. But we must not become so rooted and grounded in our plan that we argue and resist if God tries to show us a better way.

Obviously we should always have a plan to pay our bills. But the woman in this story had such an elaborate plan that it was confusing. God was trying to make the point to her that she would never enjoy her life until she began trusting Him to a greater degree. She continued:

For the rest of the day, the Holy Spirit continued to remind me when I started to plan something that He also had a plan. He showed me that by planning all the time I was trying to figure out my future by myself instead of fully depending on Him.

This woman admitted that she had a problem with independence. God does not want us to be independent or to be codependent. He wants us to be dependent on Him, because He knows that apart from Him we can do nothing (see John 15:5).

The woman ended her testimony by writing:

Not only did I experience freedom from anxiety, God completely destroyed the pattern of thinking that fostered my worry and anxiousness. I am so thankful for the truth that set me free from bondage to worry and anxiety.

This testimony contains the valuable lesson we all need to remind ourselves of: In everything that concerns us—big or small—God has a plan. Living in the fullness of that plan is much easier when we finally decide to stop striving and straining to do things on our own and surrender to God. The more we surrender to Him and to His plan, the more worry-free our lives will be.

PART 5

YOU CAN CAST
YOUR CARE

CHAPTER 20

Prayer Produces Peace, Rest, Patience, and Hope

Do not fret or have any anxiety about anything, but in every circumstance and in everything, by prayer and petition (definite requests), with thanksgiving, continue to make your wants known to God. And God's peace [shall be yours, that tranquil state of a soul assured of its salvation through Christ, and so fearing nothing from God and being content with its earthly lot of whatever sort that is, that peace] which transcends all understanding shall garrison and mount guard over your hearts and minds in Christ Jesus.

Philippians 4:6–7

Several times in this book I have mentioned the importance of casting our care upon the Lord (1 Pet. 5:7). When we hold on to the stress and cares of our lives, we end up anxious and upset. But when we let them go and allow God to take care of them, we can enter into peace. Practically speaking, though, *how* do we cast our care upon the Lord? We do it through prayer. In Philippians 4:6–7, the apostle Paul does not say, "Pray and then worry." He says, "Pray and don't worry." This is the same thing as releasing our cares to the Lord. When we do that, we end up with many blessings, including peace, rest, patience, and hope.

Prayer Produces Peace

When the enemy tries to put burdens of care on us, we are supposed to turn and give that care to God. That's a big part of what prayer is—acknowledging to the Lord that we cannot carry our burden of care, and giving it all to Him. If we pray about something and then keep on worrying about it, we are mixing a positive and a negative. The two cancel out each other, so we do not end up with the benefit we hope for.

Prayer is a positive force; worry is a negative force. I believe one reason some people operate with less power in their spiritual lives than they could have is that they cancel out their positive prayer power by giving in to the negative power of worry. Too often we pray and make positive confessions for a while, then begin to worry about a situation and make negative confessions for a while. We go back and forth between the two extremes.

As long as we pray *and worry*, we are not trusting God completely. When we pray according to His will, we need to have faith and confidence that God hears us (1 John 5:14). This kind of prayer produces peace and also leads us into rest, patience, and hope.

Prayer Produces Rest

Hebrews 4:3 says, "For we who have believed (adhered to and trusted in and relied on God) do enter that rest…." Continuing the theme of rest, Hebrews 4:9 says, "So then, there is still awaiting a full and complete Sabbath-rest reserved for the [true] people of God." The next verse goes on to say that those who have entered into God's rest have "ceased from [the weariness and pain] of human labors."

We know from Hebrews 4 that God definitely makes rest available to us. If we are not at rest, we are not truly believing Him because verse 3 clearly teaches us that the fruit of believing is rest. The kind of believing that allows us to enter into the rest of God is simple childlike faith.

A child's faith is pure and simple. When faced with a dilemma, children quickly go to their parents. They do not try to figure everything out and make detailed blueprints about how they will solve their problems. They simply believe their parents will take care of them.

For many years in my life, I claimed to be believing in God and trusting in Him. But I was not doing either of those things. I did not know the first thing about believing

God or trusting in Him. All I did was say my prayers, then worry and fret, speak negatively about my circumstances, and try to figure out everything on my own. I was anxious, panicky, irritable, and on edge constantly. Yet I said I was believing in, and trusting, God.

As believers, our rest and peace are not based on doing or achieving, but on believing in faith that God will take care of everything that concerns us. If we are really believing and trusting the Lord, we will enter into His rest. We will pray in faith and cast our cares on Him; then we will sense the perfect peace of His presence. Part of faith is also being willing to do whatever the Lord might ask us to do, but the rest He offers us is a rest in work, not from work.

Prayer Produces Patience and Hope

Romans 5:3–4 says:

Moreover [let us also be full of joy now!] let us exult and triumph in our troubles and rejoice in our sufferings, knowing that pressure and affliction and hardship produce patient and unswerving endurance. And endurance (fortitude) develops maturity of character (approved faith and tried integrity). And character [of this sort] produces [the habit of] joyful and confident hope of eternal salvation.

To say to someone, or even to ourselves, "Don't worry" is easy to do. But to actually not worry requires spiritual maturity that comes from experience with God. The more we experience the faithfulness of God, the easier it is not to worry. I also believe we must realize how useless worry is in order to give it up. Worry accomplishes nothing positive in our lives. It changes nothing for the better.

This is why continuing to have faith and trust in God, and not worrying in the midst of trials and tribulations, is vital. In hard, trying times the Lord is building in us the patience, endurance, and character that will eventually produce the habit of joyful and confident hope.

When you and I are in the midst of a spiritual battle against our enemy, every round we go through produces valuable experience and strength. Each time we resist a temptation or endure an attack, we become stronger. If we are patient through the trial and refuse to give up, sooner or later we will gain victory in the situation and enjoy increased patience, hope, and spiritual maturity in our lives. God always gives us the victory if we remain steadfast and refuse to give up.

CHAPTER 21

Trust God Completely

*Lean on, trust in, and be confident in the
Lord with all your heart and mind and
do not rely on your own insight or understanding. In all your ways know, recognize, and acknowledge Him, and He
will direct and make straight and plain
your paths.*

Proverbs 3:5–6

One reason I have always respected my husband, Dave, is that for as long as I have known
him, I have seen him cast his care upon the
Lord. In my early Christian life and ministry, I struggled to release my cares and concerns to the Lord, often living in worry and
anxiety over a situation while Dave entrusted

the matter to God and was at perfect peace about it.

Years ago, as I mentioned in Chapter 3, Dave and I lived on a very tight budget and often found ourselves wrestling with financial problems. When faced with money issues, Dave found it easy to cast those cares on the Lord, fully believing He would meet our needs. Once he left the problem with the Lord, he could relax. I often grew frustrated with him during those times because he was in the living room playing with the kids or watching television while I sat at the kitchen table poring over unpaid bills and working myself into emotional turmoil because of them. I was trying so hard to be more like Dave, to trust God and have confidence in Him, but in those days I simply did not have enough experience with God to *know* He would work out everything in His own way and in His own time.

Many Christians today can relate to what I am saying. Lots of people face financial struggles and other problems they end up worrying about. Even though these people are believers and may even be able to recite scriptures about trusting God and casting their care on Him, they still have a hard time actually doing what those verses say. They want to trust God, but cannot seem to make the leap. I can understand this because I was the same way years ago.

As I took the journey out of worry and anxiety into peace and the ability to cast my cares on the Lord, the first lesson I had to learn was to be content in the midst of my current circumstances, no matter what they were. Even if I wanted them to change—and if they really needed to change—I had to realize that I could be joyful in God even if they never changed.

I believe we get to know the Lord better during trying times than we do when everything is smooth and easy for us. These are the seasons in life that test our faith, so they are the times in which we can learn to be quiet and confident before God, allowing Him to build our trust. Paul writes: "I have learned how to be content (satisfied to the point where I am not disturbed or disquieted) in whatever state I am" (Phil. 4:11).

Paul had learned a valuable lesson, one that will benefit all of us. He knew how to be content, no matter what challenges or difficulties he had to endure. He knew how to cast his cares on the Lord and remain in the shadow of the Almighty. In spite of the many hardships he faced, Paul knew how to live day by day without letting his circumstances disturb him or take away the peace and quiet in his soul.

We can all hope and pray that we will be able to deal with things as Paul did, but if you are not there yet, do not be discouraged because Paul said it was something he *learned* to do—and learning takes time and experience. You may not yet have the ability to be content in all circumstances, but if you keep following the Lord, being faithful and obedient, and trusting in Him, then regardless of what may happen to you, sooner or later you will begin to develop the ability to be content, no matter what state you may find yourself in.

One key to being content is to trust the Lord completely, as Proverbs 3:5–6 instructed us at the beginning of this chapter. As you and I travel the road of life, we will have many opportunities to veer off our course to one side or the other. Because the enemy knows we are making progress toward our goal, he will try to distract us. He will continually tempt us to take the road of worry instead of the path of peace so he can lead us into destruction. But if we look for God's signs along the way and obey Him, we will remain within the boundaries of His guidance and protection. Instead of trying to figure out everything for ourselves, we can learn to trust the Lord to lead us in the way we should go and get us safely to our final destination.

Knowing when we are beginning to cross the boundary is not difficult. It happens when we begin to lose our peace. A loss of peace is a sure sign that we have moved out from under the protection of the shadow of the Almighty. Usually it is an indication that we have started worrying or have not repented for some type of sin or have mistreated others without acknowledging our wrong and making an effort to set things right with them. Whatever the problem may be, we need to be sensitive to our lack of peace and identify the reason for it so we can correct the problem and move back into the way of the Lord.

Proverbs 3:5–6 tells us to trust in the Lord not just with our hearts, but with our hearts *and* our minds. As we have seen, faith is the leaning of the entire personality on God in absolute trust and confidence in His power, wisdom, and goodness. When God says to lean on Him, He means totally and completely. He means we are to trust Him mentally and emotionally, as well as spiritually.

I can remember many times in the past when I *thought* I was trusting in and believing God. But mentally, I was still planning and scheming, trying to figure out how to handle everything on my own. Emotionally, I was still worrying and fretting, trying to find peace of mind and heart by keeping everything under my control. Despite the fact that I claimed to trust the Lord, I was in constant turmoil and confusion, which is always a sign that a person is headed for trouble.

I want to encourage you to be sensitive to the level of peace you feel spiritually, mentally and emotionally. When you sense the first hint of unrest, ask yourself why you may be losing your peace. Ask yourself if you have stopped fully trusting in the Lord in some way or in some specific circumstance. When you trust Him completely, you will enjoy His peace.

CHAPTER 22

Cast Your Care

Therefore humble yourselves [demote, lower yourselves in your own estimation] under the mighty hand of God, that in due time He may exalt you, casting the whole of your care [all your anxieties, all your worries, all your concerns, once and for all] on Him, for He cares for you affectionately and cares about you watchfully.

1 Peter 5:6–7

In Chapter 3, I wrote about Matthew 6:25–33 because it is such an important passage for us to understand and obey if we want to live in peace. Jesus had one more thing to say in that chapter, in its last verse. As a conclusion to everything He had taught about worry, He said: "So do not worry or be anxious about tomorrow, for tomorrow will have worries and anxieties of its own. Sufficient for each day is its own trouble" (Matt. 6:34). In other words, Jesus is telling us that each day presents us with enough to deal with, so we need to deal with each day's cares as they arise, not to borrow trouble from the next day, next week, next month, or next year.

Several times in this book I have mentioned 1 Peter 5:6–7 because I believe it is another passage of Scripture that is vital for us to know and believe if we want to enjoy worry-free living. In this chapter, I want to focus not only on the importance of casting our care on the Lord, but also on some specific ways we can do that through understanding these verses in greater detail.

One of the first things we need to understand is the meaning of the word *cast*. It refers to throwing, hurling, arising, sending, striking, thrusting, driving out, or expelling (based on definitions from W. E. Vine, Merrill Unger, and William White Jr., *Vine's*

Complete Expository Dictionary of Old and New Testament Words [Nashville: Thomas Nelson, Inc., 1984], "New Testament Section," p. 91, s.v. "CAST," A. Verbs). As you can see, the words used to describe what it means "to cast" are all rather forceful terms.

In a way, we must be forceful about casting our care on the Lord. We cannot be passive, hesitantly trying to release our cares to Him. When we feel anxious, we need to be faith-filled and confident in God. We need to be strong and courageous about throwing our cares on God with all of our might, knowing He cares for us. Casting our cares on God should be a definite decision, and enjoying God's peace should be something we are not willing to live without! We have to hurl our cares, burdens, and concerns with purpose and energy, intentionally pushing them out of our hearts and minds and casting them on God with the force a serious fisherman would use to cast a rod as far as possible. When we do that, we can rest in the conviction that He will handle our cares.

Once we understand the strength of the word *cast*, it is also helpful to understand the word *care*. I am sure you know exactly what a care is—it is simply something that matters to you. But I also want to mention a definition I came across many years ago. The Greek word translated as *care* in 1 Peter 5:7 means "to draw in different directions, distract" and signifies "that which causes this, a care, especially an anxious care" (W. E. Vine, Merrill Unger, and William White Jr., *Vine's Complete Expository Dictionary of Old and New Testament Words* [Nashville: Thomas Nelson, Inc., 1984], "New Testament Section," p. 89, s.v. "CARE" [noun and verb], CAREFUL, CAREFULLY, CAREFULNESS," A. Nouns, 1).

What do our cares do? They distract us from our fellowship with God; from the joy, peace, and rest He has for us; and from His plan for our lives. I believe the enemy's whole purpose where our cares are concerned is to cause us to lose focus on the things God wants us to pay attention to. But the Bible clearly tells us to seek God, which means to fix our focus on Him, not allowing anything or anyone to distract us.

Peter tells us to cast *all* of our cares upon the Lord—not just some of them. If anything is distracting you from your relationship with God and causing you to worry, then cast it on Him with strong determination not to take it back. Strongly refuse to allow the enemy to disrupt your fellowship with God and fill your mind with anxious thoughts about any situation or circumstance. This will lead you out of worry and into peace.

In a New Testament translation called the Worrell version (A. S. Worrell, *The Worrell New Testament* [Springfield, Mo.: Gospel Publishing House, 1980]), the footnote to 1 Peter 5:7 offers clear and powerful insight into this verse. In reference to the first part of the verse, which Worrell renders as "having cast all your anxiety on Him," the note reads:

> *The Greek tense here indicates a momentary and complete casting of one's anxiety, once for all, upon God. This, in a sense, is done when one makes a complete*

surrender of himself and his all to God for Him to manage at His will. When one puts the whole management of his life in God's hands, he may reach the place where all anxiety leaves him, regardless of the outward testings that may fall to his lot. (p. 352)

We can see from Worrell's insights that God wants to manage our lives. He wants to handle our affairs for us as a blessing to us. But sometimes we do not take advantage of the divine help that is available to us and we try to manage things on our own. When we do, often the results are not good. If we want to experience the peace of the Lord, we must learn to cast all our care upon Him—forcefully giving Him all the things that burden and distract us—permanently, not temporarily.

Can you imagine the relief you would feel if you no longer had to carry any of the burdens that seem so heavy right now? Can you begin to sense the freedom of knowing someone else is dealing with all your problems and concerns—and dealing with them in the most perfect way, the way that will be best for you? This is what happens when you cast all your care upon the Lord, realizing and believing that He truly cares for you.

CHAPTER 23

Accept Yourself

Woe to him who strives with his Maker!—a worthless piece of broken pottery among other pieces equally worthless [and yet presuming to strive with his Maker]! Shall the clay say to him who fashions it, What do you think you are making? or, Your work has no handles? Woe to him [who complains against his parents that they have begotten him] who says to a father, What are you begetting? Or to a woman, With what are you in travail? Thus says the Lord, the Holy One of Israel, and its Maker: Would you question Me about things to come concerning My children, and concerning the work of My hands [would you] command Me?

Isaiah 45:9–11

The Bible affirms that God is the One who created us. If we compare our lives to the process of making pottery, God is the Potter and "we are the clay" (Isa. 64:8). He designs, creates, molds, and shapes us according to His good plans. But sometimes we lose sight of how unique and special we are. We become frustrated with a certain physical characteristic or something in our emotional makeup. We can even end up questioning God aloud or in the privacy of our thoughts, asking, "Why did You make me this way?"

For years I did not like the way I was, the way God had put me together. I was not content with my strong, aggressive, bold personality. I wanted to be sweet, meek, and quiet because I had learned that sweet, meek, quiet people don't get in as much trouble as those who are loud and aggressive!

My personality was not the only thing I did not like. The truth is: I did not like anything about myself. I sometimes found myself asking God, "Why have You made me this way? Why do I get so upset about things when it is so easy for Dave to cast his care on you and relax? Why did You give me a such a deep voice? Why could I not have a nice, sweet, little voice like other ladies do?"

As I mentioned earlier, casting care on the Lord came easily for Dave, but that was not the case for me. It was something I had to learn. Dave had a lot more grace to cast his care, while I had to work at it. Now it comes easily for me, too, and I have learned some important lessons on my journey from worry to the peace that comes from leaving my concerns with Him. In addition to that, my voice has turned out to be a blessing. Because it is unique, it gets people's attention. I cannot even count how many people have told me they stopped changing stations on the television or radio to listen to me teaching God's Word because of the unique sound of my voice.

Years ago, though, when I prayed to God about how He had made me, I did not understand that He had a purpose in all the ways He created me. All I could do was ask why I could not be "normal" as I viewed normal at that time. I had to learn that just because I was not like everyone else I knew, I was not abnormal, I was simply unique—and so are you.

Who can say why God puts us together the way He does? But He is the Potter and we are the clay. He forms and fashions us as He does because of His infinite knowledge and because of His plan for our lives. God already knows what He is doing, but we only discover His plan by walking it out as time goes by. Our position is to trust Him.

Understanding the details of why God has made us in certain ways may take years, and in some instances we may never fully understand. Trusting God often requires some unanswered questions. We may not know all the answers, but we can learn to be content in knowing that God knows. In 1 Corinthians 13:12, Paul writes that there are some things we only know in part. We do not and cannot understand them fully. And Romans 9:21 says the potter has full rights over the clay, "to make out of the same mass (lump) one vessel for beauty and distinction and honorable use, and another for menial or ignoble and dishonorable use." The word *dishonorable* in this context does not mean dishonorable in God's eyes. It means dishonorable in the eyes of those who do not understand God's purpose. There are those who think some people are more honorable than others and certain types of work are more honorable than others, but God sees us all as equal and the only thing that is important to Him is that we serve Him joyfully in whatever He chooses for us to do.

Over the years, some people have looked at me and thought my job is more important than Dave's because I am the one in front with the microphone and on camera while Dave is behind the scenes. But each of us is in the place God has for us. We are where we are because God has placed us there. I did not ask for the position of visibility any more than Dave asked for his role behind the scenes. But we both accept the role God has assigned us and we submit ourselves to Him to mold and make us after His will and plan, not ours. Both of our jobs are equally important!

All of us have to remember that no matter what position God places us in, as long as we function in the place for which He has created us, His grace is with us. Ephesians 2:10 says:

We are God's [own] handiwork (His workmanship), recreated in Christ Jesus, [born anew] that we may do those good works which God predestined (planned beforehand) for us [taking paths which He prepared ahead of time], that we should walk in them [living the good life which He prearranged and made ready for us to live].

If we want to live in peace, we need to see ourselves as God's own handiwork and to accept the way He has made us, knowing He has a great plan for our lives.

CHAPTER 24

Six Steps to Peace

*Do not fret or have any anxiety about
anything, but in every circumstance and
in everything, by prayer and petition
(definite requests), with thanksgiving,
continue to make your wants known to
God. And God's peace...which transcends all understanding shall garrison
and mount guard over your hearts and
minds in Christ Jesus.*

Philippians 4:6–7

Sometimes, people think that casting our
care on the Lord means we do not have to do
anything except sit back and wait for God to
move in our lives. While there are times and
circumstances in which that may be true,

God often calls and expects us to do certain things as we wait for Him. One of these things is to fulfill the responsibilities He has given us.

There is a difference between casting our cares on the Lord and trying to push our responsibilities off on Him. Many times, we cast our responsibilities but keep our care—just the opposite of what God tells us to do! This will not lead us to peace; it will only create confusion. If we want to live without worry, there are at least six steps we can take, each one a specific responsibility we have as believers.

1. Trust God

I wrote at length about trusting God in Chapter 21, but I want to say a bit more here. In John 6:28, Jesus' disciples ask Him, "What are we to do, that we may [habitually] be working the works of God? [What are we to do to carry out what God requires?]" In other words, they want to know what their responsibilities are as followers of Christ.

Jesus answers in John 6:29, "This is the work (service) that God asks of you: that you believe in the One Whom He has sent [that you cleave to, trust, rely on, and have faith in His Messenger]."

The end of verse 29 could not be clearer in terms of our first responsibility as believers. We are to "cleave to, trust, rely on, and have faith in" God. Every human being has a choice—to trust in themselves, their own ideas, and their human strength, or to trust in God, His perfect wisdom, and His unlimited might. Once we choose to receive Him as Lord and Savior, we are to trust Him completely.

2. Pray without worry

All of us can encounter very intense situations in life. We may find ourselves facing a crisis in our health, a layoff at work and a lack of finances as a result, trouble with a child or family member, or some other circumstance that feels frightening or overwhelming. As human beings, we naturally worry about those things. But as believers, we have the responsibility to pray about them, cast our cares on the Lord, and *not* worry.

When we worry, we are not trusting God—and trust is the first step to peace. If we trust Him completely, we will pray about our situations and then be confident that He will handle them in the best possible way, in His perfect timing. When we believe that, we can pray and then move forward in our lives with faith instead of worry.

3. Avoid works of the flesh

When we go beyond our responsibility to pray and not worry, then our actions can become works of the flesh. We are no longer praying in faith and trusting God with the outcome. Instead, we are praying and then getting involved in what we need to leave to God, attempting to change things with our own efforts and energy.

God is not against *work*. He is against *works*. *Work* is doing by the grace of God what He has called us to do. It is the expending of our energy and effort to see God's will come to pass in our lives. But the term *works* refers to doing by our own strength and abilities what we want done. It is exerting ourselves to try to make happen what only God can do.

Some of the works of the flesh that keep us from the peace God wants us to have include worrying, reasoning, and trying to manipulate circumstances according to our personal desires and timing. The enemy uses these and other works of the flesh to rob us of our peace and joy because he wants us to be worried, upset, and confused, while God wants us to be peaceful, happy, and at rest in our souls.

As I mentioned in Chapter 6, the opposite of works is grace. If we resist the works of the flesh and rest in God, He will do everything we need Him to do in our lives.

4. Wait in obedience

Jesus' first recorded miracle took place while He attended a wedding celebration. When the hosts ran out of wine to serve their guests,

Jesus' mother, Mary, asked Him to do something about the situation. Then she said to the servants around them, "Whatever He says to you, do it" (John 2:5).

Jesus directed them to fill several large pots with water. When they had done so, He told them to draw water from the vessels. When they did, they saw that it had turned into wine, better wine than the hosts had served previously! Because of their obedience and the miracle that followed, God's greatness and power were openly displayed and Jesus' disciples learned to trust in Him (see John 2:11).

If you need some kind of breakthrough in your life, make sure you are being obedient to whatever God tells you to do and then wait in patient confidence to see what He will do. Galatians 6:9 says, "And let us not lose heart and grow weary and faint in acting nobly and doing right, for in due time and at the appointed season we shall reap, if we do not loosen and relax our courage and faint."

Sometimes when things are not working out the way we think they should or we are not getting answers as quickly as we would like, we start to think, *Why should I continue to obey God if it isn't working?* In these situations, we have to remember that God is always working, and according to Galatians 6:9, patient obedience always brings a harvest.

5. Continue to bear good fruit

In circumstances when we find ourselves having to wait on God much longer than desired, we need to continue to bear good fruit. We should be like a tree planted by the water, drawing strength and life from its source because its roots go deep into the ground (see Jer. 17:8). Even in times of drought (which can symbolize times we cannot see God moving in our lives), such a tree will continue to bear good fruit.

When we are going through difficulties, sometimes we feel we have a license to be frustrated or afraid and maybe even to be unkind to other people because we are under so much pressure. This is not true. We are not to give in to such evil tendencies (see

James 4:6). Instead, we are to bear the good fruit of the Spirit: love, joy, peace, patience, kindness, goodness, faithfulness, gentleness, and self-control (see Gal. 5:22–23).

6. Praise God

Hebrews 13:15 says, "Through Him, therefore, let us constantly and at all times offer up to God a sacrifice of praise, which is the fruit of lips that thankfully acknowledge and confess and glorify His name." This is what we are to do when we are tempted to feel anxious or upset. While we are waiting for God to answer our prayers and do what needs to be done in our lives, we are to speak words of praise that come from thankful, faith-filled hearts. The more we praise Him, the more we focus on His love and kindness toward us—and the less we have time to think about our problems.

No matter what happens, our responsibility as believers is not to fret or take matters into our own hands. Instead, we are to trust God, pray without worry, avoid works of the flesh, stay obedient, continue to bear good fruit, and to praise God in every situation. Don't focus on what you don't have, but instead be aggressively thankful for the many blessings that you do have.

CONCLUSION

Now that you have reached the end of this book, I pray you have begun to live at a whole new level of peace and are experiencing what it means to be anxious for nothing. The more peace you have in your heart, the more you can enjoy your everyday life.

Most of the time, when God begins to change us, that change takes place over a period of time as we become more and more established in the truth that sets us free. I believe with all my heart that the only way to experience lasting change and freedom is to know and live by the Word of God. As we conclude this book, I want to remind you of several key scriptures, truths from God's Word that will totally transform you as you memorize them, meditate on them, and apply them to your life.

Be anxious for nothing, but in everything by prayer and supplication with thanksgiving let your requests be made known to God. And the peace of God, which surpasses all comprehension, will guard your hearts and your minds in Christ Jesus.

Philippians 4:6–7 NASB

Therefore humble yourselves under the mighty hand of God, that He may exalt you at the proper time, casting all your anxiety on Him, because He cares for you.

1 Peter 5:6–7 NASB

Thus says the Lord: Cursed [with great evil] is the strong man who trusts in and relies on frail man, making weak [human] flesh his arm, and whose mind and heart turn aside from the Lord.... [Most] blessed is the man who believes in, trusts in, and relies on the Lord, and whose hope and confidence the Lord is.

Jeremiah 17:5–7

He Who began a good work in you will continue until the day of Jesus Christ [right up to the time of His return], developing [that good work] and perfecting and bringing it to full completion in you.

Philippians 1:6

Peace I leave with you; My [own] peace I now give and bequeath to you. Not as the world gives do I give to you. Do not let your hearts be troubled, neither let them be afraid. [Stop allowing yourselves to be agitated and disturbed; and do not permit yourselves to be fearful and intimidated and cowardly and unsettled.]

John 14:27

Come to Me, all you who labor and are heavy-laden and overburdened, and I will cause you to rest. [I will ease and relieve and refresh your souls.] Take My yoke upon you and learn of Me, for I am gentle (meek) and humble (lowly) in heart, and you will find rest (relief and ease and refreshment and recreation and blessed quiet) for your souls.

Matthew 11:28–29

He who dwells in the secret place of the Most High shall remain stable and fixed under the shadow of the Almighty [Whose power no foe can withstand]. I will say of the Lord, He is my Refuge and my Fortress, my God; on Him I lean and rely, and in Him I [confidently] trust!

Psalm 91:1–2

Lean on, trust in, and be confident in the Lord with all your heart and mind and do not rely on your own insight or understanding. In all your ways know, recognize, and acknowledge Him, and He will direct and make straight and plain your paths.

Proverbs 3:5–6

Therefore I tell you, stop being perpetually uneasy (anxious and worried) about your life, what you shall eat or what you shall drink; or about your body, what you shall put on. Is not life greater [in quality] than food, and the body [far above and more excellent] than clothing?

Matthew 6:25

But seek (aim at and strive after) first of all His kingdom and His righteousness (His way of doing and being right), and then all these things taken together will be given you besides.

Matthew 6:33

Do you have a real relationship with Jesus?

God loves you! He created you to be a special, unique, one-of-a-kind individual, and He has a specific purpose and plan for your life. And through a personal relationship with your Creator—God—you can discover a way of life that will truly satisfy your soul.

No matter who you are, what you've done, or where you are in your life right now, God's love and grace are greater than your sin—your mistakes. Jesus willingly gave His life so you can receive forgiveness from God and have new life in Him. He's just waiting for you to invite Him to be your Savior and Lord.

If you are ready to commit your life to Jesus and follow Him, all you have to do is ask Him to forgive your sins and give you a fresh start in the life you are meant to live. Begin by praying this prayer...

Lord Jesus, thank You for giving Your life for me and forgiving me of my sins so I can have a personal relationship with You. I am sincerely sorry for the mistakes I've made, and I know I need You to help me live right.

Your Word says in Romans 10:9, "If you declare with your mouth, 'Jesus is Lord,' and believe in your heart that God raised him from the dead, you will be saved" (NIV). I believe You are the Son of God and confess You as my Savior and Lord. Take me just as I am, and work in my heart, making me the person You want me to be. I want to live for You, Jesus, and I am so grateful that You are giving me a fresh start in my new life with You today.

I love You, Jesus!

It's so amazing to know that God loves us so much! He wants to have a deep, intimate relationship with us that grows every day as we spend time with Him in prayer and Bible study. And we want to encourage you in your new life in Christ.

Please visit joycemeyer.org/salvation to request Joyce's book *A New Way of Living*, which is our gift to you. We also have other free resources online to help you make progress in pursuing everything God has for you.

Congratulations on your fresh start in your life in Christ! We hope to hear from you soon.

ABOUT THE AUTHOR

JOYCE MEYER is one of the world's leading practical Bible teachers. Her daily broadcast, *Enjoying Everyday Life*, airs on hundreds of television networks and radio stations worldwide.

Joyce has written more than 100 inspirational books. Her bestsellers include *Power Thoughts*; *The Confident Woman*; *Look Great, Feel Great*; *Starting Your Day Right*; *Ending Your Day Right*; *Approval Addiction*; *How to Hear from God*; *Beauty for Ashes*; and *Battlefield of the Mind*.

Joyce travels extensively, holding conferences throughout the year and speaking to thousands around the world.

JOYCE MEYER MINISTRIES ADDRESSES

Joyce Meyer Ministries

P.O. Box 655
Fenton, MO 63026
USA
(636) 349-0303

Joyce Meyer Ministries—Canada

P.O. Box 7700
Vancouver, BC V6B 4E2
Canada
(800) 868-1002

Joyce Meyer Ministries— Australia

Locked Bag 77
Mansfield Delivery
Centre

Queensland 4122
Australia
(07) 3349 1200

Joyce Meyer Ministries—England

P.O. Box 1549
Windsor SL4 1GT
United Kingdom
01753 831102

Joyce Meyer Ministries—South Africa

P.O. Box 5
Cape Town 8000
South Africa
(27) 21-701-1056

OTHER BOOKS BY JOYCE

The Confident Woman Devotional
Ending Your Day Right*
Hearing from God Each Morning
Love Out Loud
New Day, New You
The Power of Being Thankful
Power Thoughts Devotional
Starting Your Day Right*
Trusting God Day By Day

*Also available in Spanish